WOODY GUTHRIE

Woody Guthrie is the most famous and influential folk music composer and performer in the history of the United States. His most popular song, "This Land is Your Land," has become the country's unofficial national anthem, known to every schoolchild since the 1960s. His influence is not only felt in American music, but American politics, as his music became the soundtrack to the Great Depression, and iconic of the Dust Bowl migrants. He gave voice to those who felt disenfranchised by America, yet committed to making a better life for themselves.

Here, in a short, accessible biography, bolstered with primary documents, including letters, autobiographical excerpts, and reflections by Pete Seeger, Cohen introduces Guthrie's life and musical influence to students of American history and culture.

Ronald D. Cohen is Professor Emeritus at Indiana University, Northwest. He is the author of *Folk Music: The Basics* (Routledge, 2006).

ROUTLEDGE HISTORICAL AMERICANS

SERIES EDITOR: PAUL FINKELMAN, ALBANY LAW SCHOOL

Routledge Historical Americans is a series of short, vibrant biographies that illuminate the lives of Americans who have had an impact on the world. Each book includes a short overview of the person's life and puts that person into historical context through essential primary documents, written both by the subjects and about them. A series website supports the books, containing extra images and documents, links to further research, and where possible, multi-media sources on the subjects. Perfect for including in any course on American History, the books in the Routledge Historical Americans series show the impact everyday people can have on the course of history.

Woody Guthrie: Writing America's Songs
Ronald D. Cohen

Frederick Douglass: Reformer and Statesman
L. Diane Barnes

Forthcoming:

Harry S. Truman: The Coming of the Cold War
Nicole Anslover

Sojourner Truth: Prophet of Social Justice
Isabelle Kinnard Richman

Joe Louis: Sports and Race in Twentieth Century America
Marcy Sacks

John F. Kennedy: The Burdens of Cold War Liberalism
Jason Duncan

Woodrow Wilson: Progressive President or Moral Crusader?
Kelly A. Woestman

WOODY GUTHRIE
WRITING AMERICA'S SONGS

RONALD D. COHEN

Routledge
Taylor & Francis Group

NEW YORK AND LONDON

First published 2012
by Routledge
711 Third Avenue, New York, NY 10017

Simultaneously published in the UK
by Routledge
2 Park Square, Milton Park, Abingdon, Oxon OX14 4RN

Routledge is an imprint of the Taylor & Francis Group, an informa business

Library of Congress Cataloging in Publication Data
CIP data has been applied for

ISBN: 978041589568-2 (hbk)
ISBN: 978041589569-9 (pbk)

Typeset in Minion and Scala Sans
by EvS Communication Networx, Inc.

SUSTAINABLE
FORESTRY
INITIATIVE

Certified Sourcing
www.sfiprogram.org
SFI-00555
The SFI label applies to the text stock.

Printed and bound in the United States of America by
Walsworth Publishing Company, Marceline, MO.

CONTENTS

ACKNOWLEDGMENTS

I would like to thank, in particular, Will Kaufman, as well as Ed Cray, Dave Samuelson, Hank Reineke, Bob Riesman, Michael Scully, Jim Lane, Ray Allen, Dick Weissman, Josh Dunson, Anne Koehler of the Indiana University Northwest library, and so many others for their assistance to make this book as accurate, readable, and interesting as possible. The staff of the Guthrie Archives and Publications—Tiffany Colannino, Anna Canoni, and Nora Guthrie—have been particularly cooperative and supportive, and always a delight to work with. Most helpful have been the Routledge series editor Paul Finkelman, senior history editor Kimberly Guinta, and especially editorial assistant Rebecca Novack. This is my fourth book published by Routledge and the experience has always been rewarding. Once again my wife Nancy has been my domestic support system, keeping the home fires burning as I hunch over the computer keys.

INTRODUCTION

Woody Guthrie (1912–1967) is the most famous and influential folk music composer and performer in the history of the United States. His most popular composition, "This Land Is Your Land," has become the country's unofficial national anthem, known to every school child since the 1960s. The soundtrack of the 2009 award-winning Hollywood film *Up In The Air*, starring George Clooney, begins with Sharon Jones and the Dap-Kings's updated version of the song, setting the stage for the plot to unfold. In 1998 the U.S. Postal Service issued a Woody Guthrie commemorative stamp, part of its Legends of American Music series (along with Huddie Ledbetter, Sonny Terry, and Josh White). Ten years earlier he had been inducted into the Rock and Roll Hall of Fame, and in 2000 he was granted a Grammy Lifetime Achievement Award. In 1987 Woody's "Roll On Columbia" was chosen as Washington State's official folk song, and in 2001 his "Oklahoma Hills" became Oklahoma's state folk song. In 2008 *The Live Wire: Woody Guthrie in Performance 1949* received a Grammy for Best Historical Album, and two years later Rounder Records earned a Grammy nomination for their release of *My Dusty Road*, a CD set of Woody's recordings.

On January 18, 2009, Pete Seeger, the famed folk performer and political activist, joined with Bruce Springsteen, the rock legend, to perform Woody's "This Land Is Your Land" during the "We Are One" pre-inauguration concert for President Barack Obama. While the song was familiar to most children and adults, Seeger and Springsteen included the more pointed political verses that were generally unknown, but now seemed particularly appropriate, such as: "One bright Sunday morning in the shadows of the steeple / By the Relief Office I seen my people; / As they stood there hungry, I stood there whistling; / This land was made for you and me." Seeger had first met Guthrie in early 1940 and was a close companion until his death in 1967. But Guthrie's musical legacy would live on, even as the details of his rather brief life were mostly forgotten, if ever known.[1]

Guthrie's creative energies spanned less than twenty years, from the late 1930s to the early 1950s, when Huntington's disease, a debilitating genetic disorder that affects muscle coordination and leads to an early death, mostly confined him to a hospital bed for the rest of his life. While active he was incredibly productive, however, capturing the spirit of grassroots America in his songs and stories, while always proud of his maverick personality. Growing up in Oklahoma and Texas, he spent most of his adult years in Los Angles and New York, thereby connecting rural and urban America, the farm and the city. His life was the stuff of legends, and indeed inspired the award-winning 1976 Hollywood film, *Bound For Glory*, based on Guthrie's semi-fictional autobiography of the same name. Woody Guthrie was one of a kind, but he also tried to capture the spirit of the times, particularly the Depression years of hope and struggle that gave him so much inspiration.

There are two general biographies, Joe Klein, *Woody Guthrie: A Life* (1980) and Ed Cray, *Ramblin' Man: The Life and Times of Woody Guthrie* (2004), in addition to more specialized studies, such as Mark Allen Jackson, *Prophet Singer: The Voice and Vision of Woody Guthrie* (2007) and Will Kaufman, *Woody Guthrie: American Radical* (2011). There are also edited books of essays, such as Robert Santelli and Emily Davidson, eds., *Hard Travelin': The Life and Legacy of Woody Guthrie* (1999), based on presentations at a Woody Guthrie conference at the Rock and Roll Hall of Fame in 1996; John Partington, ed., *The Life, Music and Thought of Woody Guthrie: A Critical Appraisal* (2011). In 2012 the Grammy Museum in Los Angeles, along with venues in Oklahoma and New York, will devote the year to Woody exhibits and other events, celebrating his centenary; and there will be related activities throughout the country. The Guthrie Foundation and Archives in Mt. Kisco, New York, is the repository of his papers and encourages new writing and recording projects.

A brief Woody biography, touching upon not only the highlights of his life, but also his lasting, and vivid, legacy into the twenty-first century, now seems particularly appropriate, along with the centennial of his birth in 2012. He became friends with some of the most influential musical and political figures of the time, who were crucial in furthering his career, including Pete Seeger, Alan Lomax, Lead Belly, Moses Asch, Cisco Houston, Burl Ives, Josh White, Sonny Terry, Brownie McGhee, and Will Geer—a racially mixed group that demonstrated Woody's democratic values. Coming of age during the height of the Depression, Woody began to write and perform the songs that captured these hard times, both rural and urban, while he became immersed in the current political struggles. He joined the Almanac Singers in the early 1940s, along with Pete Seeger, Lee Hays, Millard Lampell, and assorted others, performing old and new folk songs, then entered the Merchant Marine to support the war effort; at the same time he published his influential autobiography/novel *Bound For Glory*, which is still in print.

Following the war Woody continued his political activism, as well as his prolific songwriting and recording career for a few years. He easily attracted friends with his magnetic personality and sparkling wit, but he could also be a trying house guest. He had little regard for personal hygiene and acceptable table manners; he slept with his boots on and helped himself to whatever he needed. He was an irresponsible husband and father, with little thought of family responsibilities, often disappearing for months at a time, at least until his second marriage. He had little thought about money, which came and went, and he scoffed at middle-class values and morality. He was a heavy drinker, although this was often confused with the growing signs of the deadly Huntington's disease, and by the mid-1950s he was increasingly confined to a hospital bed until his death in 1967. Indeed, his productive life was short, but these were exceedingly rich and eventful years, and he would leave a powerful musical, cultural, and political legacy. Perhaps his quirky, annoying personal habits, stoked by his genetic ailment, were the key to his prolific, creative artistic achievements. Geniuses are often oddballs, and certainly Woody Guthrie fits this description.

In the 1950s Woody was virtually unknown by the general public, with little written about him and few of his songs recorded, published, or performed. Beginning with Jack Elliott, Cisco Houson, and a few others, followed by Bob Dylan's arrival in New York in 1961, his fame would spread. Indeed, Dylan not only promoted Guthrie, but sparked the importance of singer-songwriters as a key element in the folk music revival. Woody's songs would now be increasingly performed and would be enormously influential in defining folk music to a new generation. Within a few years there were countless recordings of his songs, reissues of his older recordings plus those of many others, as well as numerous songbooks. This is when "This Land Is Your Land" became so popular. A whole new generation, including Country Joe McDonald, Bruce Springsteen, and Woody's son Arlo, would carry on his legacy, with Pete Seeger continuing to be in the forefront well into the twenty-first century. Hundreds of unknown songs were discovered in the Guthrie Archives, resulting in new recordings by Billy Bragg and Wilco, as well as Hannukah songs by the Klezmatics, and assorted others. Woody had finally become not only a legend, but a monument to the force of songs in influencing social and musical movements. Moreover, scholars and journalists have published a spate of books and articles, seemingly exploring every facet of Woody's music and fascinating life.

PART I

WOODY GUTHRIE

CHAPTER 1

THE EARLY YEARS

"I hate a song that makes you think that you're not any good. I hate a song that makes you think that you are just born to lose. No good to nobody. No good for nothing. Because you are either too old or too young or too fat or too slim or too ugly or too this or too that.... Songs that run you down or songs that poke fun at you on account of your bad luck or hard traveling. I am out to fight those kinds of songs to my very last breath of air and my last drop of blood."

—Woody Guthrie

Woodrow Wilson Guthrie's father, Charley Guthrie, was born in Bell County in South Texas. In 1897 his family moved north to the Indian Territory, which would become Oklahoma, the country's forty-sixth state, a decade later. The federal government was giving 160 acres of formerly Indian land to anyone with Indian blood, and luckily Charley's step-mother was one-eighth Creek. Charley preferred to work in a store rather than farm, and while employed in J. B. Wilson's store in Castle he met the Kansas-born Nora Belle Tanner. They were married in 1904 and shared many interests, including music, with Nora doing the singing and her husband playing the guitar and banjo. Charley soon plunged into local politics, and when elected district court clerk in 1907 the family moved to the nearby town of Okemah, where selling real estate quickly led to a decent income. Woodrow Wilson Guthrie, their third child, was born on July 14, 1912, twelve days after the Democratic Party nominated Woodrow Wilson as its candidate for president (he would be elected in November). Charley was a conservative Democrat and no friend of the radical movement gaining steam in Oklahoma the year Eugene V. Debs was the Socialist Party candidate for president.

Woody had a comfortable childhood in Okemah, at least for a few years. He aptly described his hometown, with his usual long descriptive list: "Okemah was one of the singingest, square dancingest, drinkinest, yellingest, preachingest, walkingest, takingest, laughingest, cryingest, shootingest, fist fightingest, bleedingest, gamblingest, gun, club, and razor carryingest of our ranch and farm towns." When the country plunged into World War I in 1917, the state's numerous oil fields and high farm prices brought increasing prosperity until the war ended in 1918, followed by an economic crash two years later, when the government withdrew its farm price supports.[1]

The Guthrie family was now devastated and had to struggle through the 1920s, living in a series of shacks as Charley managed various odd jobs. Meanwhile, Nora was becoming increasingly erratic, even violent, in her behavior, the first signs that she had Huntington's disease, although at the time there was no explanation for what was the problem. Woody, small for his age and quite rambunctious, was mostly left to his own devices. Music came to dominate much of his early life, particularly after he obtained a harmonica when hearing George, a local African American, playing "Railroad Blues"; he often grabbed the chance to sing and dance in public. His mother was committed to the Central State Hospital for the Insane in Norman in June 1927 after seriously burning his father, so Woody was left to live with neighbors and pick up odd jobs in the community to survive. Here is Woody's account: "My sister, Clara died in the explosion of a coal oil stove. Later on, worried from this and things that added as they went, my mother's nerves gave away like an overloaded bridge. Papa tried to get back into the trading and the swapping game, but never got a new toehold."[2]

In June 1929, just about seventeen, Woody moved to Texas, to live near his father, who had recently relocated, and scratch out a living, which he would describe, although without much of his usual exaggeration: "I hit the road south to Houston, Galveston, the Gulf, and back, doing all kinds of odd jobs hoeing figs orchards picking grapes hauling wood, helping carpenters and cement men, working with water well drillers." Woody was now a self-taught painter and picked up odd jobs designing signs and sketching portraits. Then he discovered the guitar and before long was learning to play from his uncle, Jefferson Davis Guthrie, a skilled musician. He had little interest in school and dropped out of the local high school in Pampa, but was an avid reader who eagerly devoured the books in the town library. As he later recalled in *Bound For Glory*, his semi-fictional autobiography: "I wanted to be my own boss. Have my own job of work whatever it was, and be on my own hook. I walked the streets in the drift of the dust and wondered where was I bound for, where was I going what was I going to do? I went to the town library and scratched around in the books. I carried them home by the dozens and by the armloads, on any subject, I didn't care which." Indeed, he became very well self-educated.[3]

Woody's mother died in the hospital in 1930, and he was at loose ends for a few years, spending much time with his friend Matt Jennings and listening to the latest hillbilly records, particularly the Carter Family, Jimmie Rodgers, the classically trained popularizer Vernon Dalhart, and the many other popular southern musicians. Although Rodgers had died in 1933, since the late 1920s he had become the country's most popular country music performer through his recordings and public appearances. Woody might even have met him in South Texas, and later would base a few of his songs on Rodgers's blue yodels. While Woody became steeped in the old ballads as well as new country tunes, he was particularly influenced by the Carter Family—A.P., his wife Sara, and his sister-in-law Maybelle— with their more traditional vocals and church-inflected tunes. Woody began writing his own songs when he joined a local band, the Corncob Trio, with his friend Matt, as well as a family trio with his uncle Jeff. The latter appeared briefly on station WDAG in Amarillo, while the Corncob Trio had a regular morning show on KPDN in Pampa. Music had come to dominate his life, and he quickly began playing not only the guitar and harmonica, but also the mandolin, violin, drums, even the washboard: "We played for rodeos, centennials, carnivals, parades, fairs, just bust-down parties, and played several nights and days a week just to hear our own boards rattle and our strings roar around in the wind. It was along in these days I commenced singing. I guess it was singing."[4]

The economic depression, with 25 percent unemployment, had now ravaged the country, and Woody barely managed to survive while dating Matt's younger sister, Mary. They married on October 28, 1933, not long after President Franklin Roosevelt entered the White House and launched the New Deal. But the Guthries were little affected by the Democratic takeover of the federal government. As Woody would explain: "I married a fine Irish girl by the name of Mary Jennings and we lived in the ricketiest of the oil town shacks long enough to have no clothes, no money, no groceries and two children, both girls."[5]

Woody and Mary's first child, Gwendolyn, known as "Teeny," arrived in November 1935, not long after the great dust storm roared through Texas in April, which inspired Woody's song "The Texas Dust Storms." There would soon be two others, another daughter, Sue, born in 1937, and their son, Bill, born in 1939. He now published his first songbook, *Alonzo M. Zilch's Own Collection of Original Songs and Ballads.* Busy with his music, painting, and family responsibilities, he yet felt the urge to travel and in 1936 began to roam around, joining thousands of other rootless boys, men, and some women, while picking up odd jobs: "I hit the highway to look around for a place for us to go. I carried my pockets full of paint brushes and my guitar slung across my back." In early 1937, while still in Pampa, he crafted a thoughtful letter for his newborn niece Mary Ann Guthrie, the daughter of Woody's brother Roy. "Love principles," he wrote in his best grammar. "Not people. Love equal and impartial. Love for love's sake. For God is love. Hate nobody. Harm no living thing. Live to help and to serve always. Think. Do your own of this."[6]

Parts of Oklahoma, Texas, and the surrounding states in the middle of the country began experiencing a severe drought in 1930, which lasted through much of the decade. This was coupled with the extensive cultivation of the land beginning in World War I that stripped the top soil and uprooted the grasses, leading to extensive erosion and the creation of what become known as the Dust Bowl. Circumstances were ripe for the great dust storms that began in South Dakota in 1933, followed by a monster two-day storm in May 1934—the dust carried as far as Chicago, Boston, and New York City—and culminating on April 14, 1935, "Black Sunday," that Guthrie would document in his songs and stories. The sun was blocked and visibility reduced to almost zero throughout the day, with dust covering everything. The drought—combined with the economic disaster of the Depression throughout the decade, with millions left jobless and homeless—dislocated over 2.5 million, with around 200,000 moving to California.

Generally known as Okies, although they came from Texas, Arkansas, and other central states as well as Oklahoma, these uprooted migrants faced numerous problems when they arrived in California, with many heading for Los Angeles. The hard times created a fear among the settled white population and much of the business community of competition for the scarce jobs, particularly from those who many considered inferiors. Prejudice and the segregation of African Americans, Mexicans, Japanese, as well as the Chinese had long been widespread in California, but the new white arrivals sparked added hostilities. Rural white southerners (hillbillies) had often been typed in the North as mental and social inferiors, along with immigrants from Eastern and Southern Europe (Catholic, Jewish, and Orthodox), and now they were lumped with the destitute from the Midwest, considered dull and shiftless. Such attitudes were reinforced by the dubious "scientific" findings of the eugenics movement of the time, which differentiated between ethnic and racial groups, with the Okies often considered as something less than traditional whites. Popular magazines, comics, and Hollywood films often reinforced such crude, rural stereotypes, for example the Li'l Abner cartoon character.

Woody arrived in California in 1937 in the midst of such hostile feelings by the state's white establishment. Joining with his cousin, Jack Guthrie, a polished cowboy singer, the two wound up in Los Angeles, and soon landed a job on the local radio station KFVD. *The Oklahoma and Woody Show* began on the morning of July 19 and was an immediate hit with the Okie transplants. Woody loved the place. "The radio station was full of all kinds of sound effects. There were thunder machines, lightning machines, inner sanctum squeaky doors and electric organs, coconut shell devices," his friend Lee Hays would relate. "Woody would wander around the studio rattling and banging and shaking on these things, just having a hell of a good time" when not on the air.[7]

California's recent immigrants had become a prime audience for country music. Many others, however, had been stopped at the state's border, unable to enter because they were too poor, an official policy enforced by the Los Angeles police until it was abandoned not long before Woody arrived; the cruel practice was the target of Woody's song "Do-Re-Mi," which warned the migrants that if they didn't have enough money they would be refused entry. Various radio stations featured local country and western performers, such as the Stuart Hamblen Gang, the Beverly Hillbillies, the Bronco Busters, and the Sons of the Pioneers, who also gave numerous concerts and increasingly appeared on records. Moreover, Gene Autry, a popular recording star, beginning in 1934 had become the most famous of the growing number of movie singing cowboys. Woody had now found a musical home. His young friend Maxine Crissman joined the duo on KFVD in August, and became Woody's permanent partner in mid-September 1937 when Jack left.

Born in Missouri, Maxine and her family had moved to Los Angeles in 1932; she graduated from high school the next year and began working in the local garment industry until connecting with Woody. Very popular in their morning spot, the first *Woody and Lefty Lou* show—Woody had renamed Maxine "Lefty Lou from Old Mizzou"—opened with the duo singing two songs, including Woody's "Curly-Headed Baby." They quickly developed into a creative act of music and humor, featuring many of his new songs, such as "Do-Re-Mi" and "Philadelphia Lawyer," about a city slicker who is shot by a cowboy for making love to his wife. They appeared at various local public events, as well as twice a day, six days a week on KFVD. They also distributed the mimeographed booklet "Woody and Lefty Lou's Favorite Collection [of] Old Time Hillbilly Songs," a common practice of country and cowboy performers. "Lefty Lou and me took quite a hand in politics and sung some of our first political and religious songs of our own making right then and there," Woody would recall. Not all of their songs were political, however, but some referred to the dignity of the rural poor. Now with a slight income, he arranged for Mary, Gwendolyn, and their four- month-old daughter Sue to move to Los Angeles in November, although they would soon return to Texas.[8]

Woody's vaguely liberal politics were still quite unformed in early 1938 when KFVD station owner J. Frank Burke's father, Burke Senior, launched *Light,* a weekly paper that promoted the campaign of Culbert Olson for governor. Frank Merriam, the current conservative governor, had won in a very nasty contest in 1934 against the socialist and popular writer Upton Sinclair, the author of *The Jungle.* Woody began a "Cornbread Philosophy" column for the paper, supporting the liberal Olson, who won for governor in 1938. He also backed the Ham and Eggs state legislative initiative, which proposed issuing the elderly thirty dollars in script to improve their consumer spending by increasing their incomes—Social Security did not yet exist and many had no private pension plan—performing such songs as "Give Us That Old Age Pension" and "Ham and Eggs Is Moving On," based on the tune for the "Battle Hymn of the Republic." When the plan lost in 1938 he published the pamphlet *$30 Dollars Wood Help!,* but it was again defeated in November 1939.

Maxine left the "Woody and Lefty Lou" program in June 1938, and for a while Woody had his own show. But he soon took off as the *Light*'s "hobo correspondent," roaming through the Hoovervilles (homeless camps named after former president Herbert Hoover) and migrant worker camps of Northern California, singing along the way and sharpening his anger as he witnessed the terrible plight of the dust bowl refugees: "I sung songs for the cotton pickers and cotton strikers, and for migratory workers, packers, canning house workers, fruit pickers, and all sorts of other country and city workers." Upon returning his show was named *Woody, The Lone Wolf.* Drawing upon his hardscrabble life, he had now developed a rustic persona for his radio shows and public appearances. Still, he was highly self-educated and could turn on and off this folksy style when appropriate throughout his life. He proved a gifted actor. He also demonstrated that there was definitely an audience for his developing left-wing political views.[9]

In the early 1930s labor unrest and the obvious plight of the newly arriving migrants had begun to attract much attention, not only from the state's increasingly worried elites, but also from academics. Paul Taylor, a labor economist at the University of California-Berkeley, had begun to study the situation, and was soon joined by Dorothea Lange, a photographer in San Francisco. They began traveling around the state documenting the increasing poverty, and by July 1935 Lange's vivid photographs accompanying Taylor's detailed descriptions were circulated in an article for the *Survey Graphic* magazine. They documented the story soon brought to a wider audience in John Steinbeck's popular novel *The Grapes of Wrath* in

1939, released as a feature film the following year. In 1936 Taylor and Lange spread their research into the South and West, resulting in the book *An American Exodus,* also published in 1939. During this time Lange worked for the Farm Security Administration's photography unit when she produced her most famous photograph, "Migrant Mother." Moreover, the attorney and journalist Carey McWilliams published *Factories in the Field* in 1939, still another depiction of the sordid plight of the migrant farmers.

Woody was not the first to capture and broadcast the troubles of the rural dispossessed, but he was surely the first to use songs, such as "Dust Pneumonia Blues," "I Ain't Got No Home in This World Anymore," "Dust Bowl Refugee," and "So Long, It's Been Good to Know You," which ended, "This dusty old dust is a getting my home, and I've got to be drifting along." The most commercially successful of these songs was "Oklahoma Hills," which became a national hit with his cousin Jack Guthrie's recording in 1945 for Capitol Records. After Jack's record was out, Woody had to inform Capitol that he, not Jack, was the author and so deserved the copyright and royalties, which he got. Gene Autry featured "Oklahoma Hills" in his 1946 film *Sioux City Sue* for Republic Pictures, and there were also recordings by country performers Johnny Bond, T. Texas Tyler, Bob Wills, and Ernest Tubb, as well as the band leader Bob Crosby with the Dinning Sisters. These early tunes mostly lacked political bite, since Woody's understanding of the larger issues was just forming. Woody liked to pride himself on being a lone wolf, a maverick, with no strings attached, but there were always friends who aided and guided his musical and political life.

In Los Angeles, for example, he met Ed Robbin and through him Will Geer, who quickly exposed Woody to the developing world of radical politics. Geer was a struggling New York actor, originally from Indiana, who had arrived in Los Angeles in 1932, moved back to New York, then returned to Los Angeles in 1939. Geer appeared in the interracial play *Stevedore,* directed by Ed Robbin, in late 1934. By 1938 Robbin's left-wing politics had led him to become the Los Angeles bureau chief and sole reporter for the *People's World,* the West Coast's organ for the Communist Party. He also had a daily news commentary on KFVD beginning in 1937.

The Communist Party of the United States (CPUSA) had emerged in 1919, following the downfall of the Russian monarchy, the triumph of the Communist Party, and the subsequent formation of the Soviet Union following World War I. Because of fears of radicalism, however, the federal government persecuted the members of the CPUSA, which was essentially driven underground for some years. Struggling through the 1920s, riven by factional disputes and government harassment, the CPUSA emerged in the early 1930s when the onset of the Depression led many to look for radical alternatives to the country's current economic and social problems. The leadership of the party, located in New York City, where the party organ, *The Daily Worker*, was published, had close ties to the international Communist Party based in Moscow, but within the United States there was some local autonomy. The *People's World* felt far enough from New York to develop its own agenda, although within the general framework of the party's leadership and goals. The party had pursued a strategy of non-cooperation with other parties on the left, such as the Socialist Party, until 1935, when the rise of Mussolini's Fascism in Italy and Hitler's Nazis party in Germany, combined with the continuing economic depression, led the party to create a Popular Front by aligning itself with people who were not communists but who agreed with the party on some issues. In this period the CPUSA created a number of organizations—later known as Communist fronts—that non-communists could join which would in fact be run by CPUSA members and exist to support the party's agenda. The popular front included not only socialists but also many connected with Roosevelt's New Deal political agenda, some of whom never knew that the organizations they supported or joined were fronts for the CPUSA. The CPUSA also worked within the emerging new industrial union, the Congress of Industrial Organizations (CIO), composed of workers in heavy industries, such as the steel, rubber, and auto manufacturing.

Most Communist Party members had some allegiance to the Soviet Union, but, which was more important, they supported labor unions, combated racism and segregation, fought for equal justice, called for a socialist economic system (i.e., strong government involvement in the economy), and battled fascism at home and abroad. The party attracted tens of thousands of members and supporters, particularly among the country's intellectuals, labor organizers, artists, teachers, writers, and actors, who were searching for an alternative economic and social system in the midst of the current economic disaster.

Woody accidentally ran into Ed Robbin at KFVD in 1938 and they soon became close friends. "We met at the station daily, and he frequently came to the house," Robbin would recall. "There, he would sit in the backyard picking out tunes or talking and playing with our children.... I became an informal booking agent for him." At the time Woody was not a dutiful father for his own children, but he had begun to write the clever children's songs that would be a vital part of his musical legacy. Woody had also begun to contribute some personal thoughts under the title "Woody Sez" for the local *United Progressive News,* which soon became his regular column in the *People's World* because of Robbin's connections. From May 1939 until early 1940, he produced over 170 columns. They were written in his folksy hill-country dialect. He also contributed eighty-two clever cartoons that appeared on page one of the paper and referred to his column on page four, illustrating his sense of humor and artistic bent.[10]

His sister Mary Jo later would comment on his creative side: "Woody never sent store-bought greeting cards. And I like to think he did not write letters, he created them. He crafted them on flattened paper sacks, paper towels, Christmas wrapping paper, the backs of programs for his performances, on the margins of each page of a song book he published in the 1940s, and anything else he could find. Family members grew accustomed to receiving his artistic letters and cards. They not only kept us aware of his comings and goings, but provided keepsakes that show the depth of his creativity."[11]

Woody would never join the Communist Party, because he was too much of a maverick to follow a strict party line, but he long supported its social and political agenda, while remaining lukewarm about the virtues of the Soviet Union, except while they were an ally during World War II. He believed in causes more than organizations. Later he would join the left-wing National Maritime Union (NMU) as well as the loosely formed People's Songs musical organization in the 1940s because of their goals and commitments, but only conforming according to his own proclivities. "He didn't bother to read what Karl Marx had written, or Lenin," Robbin explained. "Woody believed that what is important is the struggle of the working people to win back the earth, which is rightfully theirs. He believed that people should love one another and organize into one big union."[12]

Through his friends Ed Robbin and Will Geer, Woody found himself immersed in various left-wing political causes. "I saw this wonderful combination of a fellow who wrote his own poetry every day and sang it every day," Geer later commented. "And I said to myself, what a sorry fish I am. All I do is take words from someone else and say them over and over again. Here was a guy who was creating, even though his things seemed kind of monotonous to me in those days.... He was talking about changing things, making them better." During the summer and fall of 1939, Woody toured California's migrant worker camps with Geer, working for the John Steinbeck Committee to Aid Farm Workers, performing for the struggling farmers, before Will and his wife Herta returned to New York in November. Woody later wrote about California: "I saw the hundreds of thousands of stranded, broke, hungry, idle, miserable people that lined the highways all out through the leaves and underbrush. I heard these people sing in their jungle camps and in their Federal Work Camps and sang songs I made up for them over the air waves."[13]

Geer's connections helped Woody meet various Hollywood actors, including Melvyn Douglas and Eddie Albert, as well as the writer John

Steinbeck, but he was not much taken with celebrities, although he charmed them all. The Hollywood film colony had a vibrant political culture, which somewhat included Woody. He felt more at home with the skid row bums and homeless migrants, however. Soon after losing his job on KFVD in November 1939, now dead broke—he was never able to save money— Woody, Mary, and their three children (a boy, Bill, had just been born) returned to Pampa, Texas: "I thought that if I could drift back towards New York and get myself a fresh new start, things might run smoother. So Mary, Sue, Teeny, Bill and me took off across the rims and edges of the Two Thousand Mile Desert to crawl and sweat and ache and pound back again to our little shack house in Texas." But Woody was itching to continue on the road. Geer, now starring as Jeeter Lester in the hit Broadway play *Tobacco Road,* had written to Woody inviting him to New York and a possible part in the production. Despite his growing family, he did not hesitate to take off for New York City. He would have little contact with them from now on. Woody and Mary finally divorced in 1943, by which time she worked and had her own income, since she could never depend on his financial support.[14]

On February 16, 1940, Guthrie arrived in the snow-covered city after a painful trip, partly spent hitchhiking in the bitter cold. He quickly moved into the Geers's apartment. "He asked me, so I told him we were paying $250 for the month for this apartment," Will would recall. "At first he thought it was $250 for the rest of the year. He was so upset when he found out that he went down to the Bowery to sleep around and said he wanted to find out the difference between the rich and the poor." Woody did not appear in *Tobacco Road*, but Will managed to get him some singing jobs, beginning at a benefit for Spanish Civil War refugees at the Mecca Temple auditorium.[15]

Woody could be a heavy drinker, and Will worried about his seemingly drunken behavior. Some of Woody's apparent drunkenness was surely an early symptom of Huntington's disease, however. Woody was a difficult house guest in a small New York apartment—he was always careless about his surroundings or other people's property—and he did not stay long with the Geers. About a week after he arrived, he moved to a seedy hotel, but not before he penned a ballad, "I Don't Feel at Home on the Bowery No More," a version of "I Ain't Got No Home." Despite their close, and lifelong, friendship, Woody's rough manners were a bit too much, even for the Geers, and they were somewhat relieved to see him go.

Woody's introduction to the city's active left-wing and folk music communities came on March 3, 1940, at the "Grapes of Wrath" midnight benefit for the Steinbeck Committee to Aid Farm Workers, which Geer had arranged at the Forrest Theater, where *Tobacco Road* was still being performed. The gala musical event featured, besides Woody, the southern mountain singer-songwriter Aunt Molly Jackson, the African American performers Huddie "Lead Belly" Ledbetter, the Golden Gate Quartet, and Josh White, as well as Burl Ives and Pete Seeger—roots musicians (except Seeger and Ives) who would play important roles in the folk revival. The young Alan Lomax, Assistant in Charge of the Archive of American Folk Song at the Library of Congress, was also there. This landmark event, with a racially mixed, dynamic lineup, would inaugurate Guthrie's friendships with Lomax, Seeger, Lead Belly, and so many others. Ethnic and racial diversity appealed to Woody, a sign of his left-wing politics. Pete Seeger had known about Woody since the previous year, when Geer wrote to him, "I've met a great ballad singer named Woody Guthrie. You got to meet him, I'm trying to persuade him to go to New York." Geer then sent a copy of Woody's mimeographed songbook, *On a Slow Train to California*. For Seeger, "Woody was the star of the show," thanks to Geer. Pete Seeger was just beginning his stellar musical career and longtime friendship with Woody.[16]

New York was America's cultural capital, having long attracted writers, dancers, singers, artists, musicians, actors, as well as all sorts of political activists. The country's major recording studios and radio stations were located here, as were the premier legitimate theaters and publishing houses, while Greenwich Village remained a haven for cultural non-conformists. A colorful character such as Woody, while somewhat at sea in Los Angeles, now found a welcoming home, nurturing social/political environment, and a raft of new friends, including an interracial group of traditional and influential musicians.

Aunt Molly Jackson, for one, born in Kentucky in 1880 and the wife of a coal miner, had composed "Ragged Hungry Blues," which she performed in 1931 for the popular writers John Dos Passos, Theodore Dreiser, and others who were in Kentucky investigating the wretched conditions in the coal mines and towns. She soon moved to New York and connected with the activist community. For a while she traveled the country raising funds for the miners, but by decade's end was living in poverty on the Lower East Side, although still a powerful singer and songwriter.

Huddie "Lead Belly" Ledbetter became another close friend. Born in Mooringsport, Louisiana, in 1889, after a checkered career as an itinerant musician, while spending many years in prisons in Texas and Louisiana, in 1933 he was discovered by the folklorists John and Alan Lomax, and the following year left prison to work for John Lomax. He now moved to New York and began an active life of recording and performing, becoming highly influential within folk music circles. Lead Belly and Woody became close friends. "As Woody was so often an older protective guy with younger singers, Leadbelly [sic] was always kind of fatherly and protective of Woody in Leadbelly's house," Lee Hays would later explain. "It was always a place where Woody could go and did go often for food and a place to sleep and probably give Martha, Huddie's wife, fits, the way he did other people when he hung out at their houses.... They sang together. I remember one wonderful evening when the two of them played four-handed piano on the old Almanac piano we had given Huddie, and banged the hell out of it until the neighbors made him stop. They used to swap verses on songs, blues verses too, which Woody always loved to do." This happened at a time when the country's musicians and music industry were heavily segregated along racial lines.[17]

Saunders "Sonny" Terry, a blind harmonica player, had been born in North Carolina in 1911, while his long-time partner, the talented guitar player Walter "Brownie" McGhee, born in 1915, had been raised in Tennessee but moved to North Carolina in the late 1930s. The African American duo finally met in 1940 and soon became part of New York's left-wing cultural movement. As for Burl Ives, born in 1909, he had grown up in Illinois, and moved to New York by the early 1940s. With his piercing voice and knowledge of traditional songs, he quickly developed a growing audience. The deft blues performer Josh White, born in 1914 in South Carolina, had a difficult musical apprenticeship, but he arrived in New York in 1932 and launched a prolific recording career.

Besides this group of stellar musicians, who would quickly become Woody's friends and musical companions, Pete Seeger, who settled in New York in 1940, and Alan Lomax were vital to his life and musical career. Born in 1919, the son of the noted musicologist Charles Seeger, whose family had arrived in the colonies before the Revolutionary War, Pete had briefly attended Harvard College, then dropped out to make his way in the world. He was steeped in music, particularly playing the 5-string banjo, and had worked with Alan Lomax at the Library of Congress, where he developed a wealth of knowledge of traditional tunes. Lomax, the son of the folklorist John Lomax, a white southerner, was born in Texas in 1915 and at an early age joined his father on collecting trips through the South, when they first met Lead Belly in 1933. At the young age of twenty-one he began working for the Library of Congress, and in 1937 became the head of the Archive of American Folk Song, where he remained until 1942. During this period he conducted numerous recording trips throughout much of the country, while also having his own radio shows on CBS, and promoting many of his friends, such as Lead Belly, Josh White, Burl Ives, and Pete Seeger. Along with his older supporters Will Geer and Ed Robbin, Guthrie's career heavily depended on Seeger, Lomax, and his growing circle of musical and political friendships.

Woody was also writing his column for the *People's World,* which continued from March to November 1940, as well as a new series for the *Daily Worker* during the same period. He loved roaming New York's derelict neighborhoods, then writing about his experiences. "He'd come up to see me after the show, *Tobacco Road,*" Geer recalled. "He must have see[n] that show forty times. And he'd come up and pick me up after the last act, and we'd walk over about three or four blocks down to the docks, and there'd be one bar where nothing but the British sailors hung out, another bar where the French sailors were, all during the war years, back and forth, you know." Both Geer and Guthrie kept busy performing for various left-wing organizations and just running around the city. A second "Grapes of Wrath" evening on April 12, 1940, sponsored by the Oklahoma Aid Committee, included Geer, Guthrie, and the performer Tony Kraber. The close friends both appeared in a musical event in November 1940, noted in the *Sunday Worker* as a "folk expression of anti-war feeling voiced in the songs of the American people." The city was alive with musical shows and political cabarets, such as Café Society, with a mix of comedy, jazz, blues, folk music, and topical songs.[18]

Joseph Stalin's Soviet Union and Adolph Hitler's Nazi Germany signed a nonaggression pact in late August 1939, then both invaded Poland in September and initiated World War II in Europe. The official Communist Party line now shifted from intervention against the fascists (Germany and Italy) in Europe to maintaining neutrality. Large numbers of the party's members and supporters reacted bitterly against this surprising move and dropped their support, but others, such as Woody—although not a party member, he often agreed with the leadership's position—accepted the new line. The American Youth Congress, allied with the CPUSA, held its convention in February 1940 in the nation's capital, and the delegates, invited by the president's wife, Eleanor Roosevelt, stood outside the White House demanding jobs and peace. To honor the demonstrators, Woody quickly penned the peace song "Why Do You Stand There in the Rain?," which was published as sheet music by the Modern Record Company and appeared in the *Daily Worker* on April 18, 1940: "Now the guns in Europe roar as they have so oft before. / And the war lords play the same old game again."[19]

Peace songs had a long history, usually written before or after a war; such was the case in World War I. The American League Against War and Fascism had been formed in 1933, and changed its name to the American League for Peace and Democracy (ALPD) in 1937, uniting various groups on the left in a broad peace coalition. While the peace movement was heating up by mid-decade, the organized left, including those in and around the Communist Party, were mostly turning out songs supporting labor unions and the working class. Numerous labor song books were published, but those filled with peace songs were quite rare, except for the Student Peace Union's *Patters For Peace*. Similar to many of the left-wing songbooks of the time, however, many of the SPU's songs were difficult to sing, apparently not connected with any familiar tunes, and only one included music.

The Theatre Arts Committee (TAC) was formed in 1938, an alliance of left-wing film, theater, and radio entertainers, and for almost two years staged a variety of politically charged shows. TAC published a monthly magazine and promoted a variety of recordings, radio shows, and a weekly cabaret in New York, with a heavy anti-Nazi flavor, but with an antiwar message as well. The TAC Radio Division wrote and published "It Shall Not Come To Pass," probably in 1939, with the refrain, "We, who are this nation say: We will not go to war / We have said it oft before; / But now we command it! / It Shall Not Come To Pass!"[20]

On February 23, 1940, Woody also wrote what eventually became his most famous song, "This Land Is Your Land," his reaction to the mushy sentiments of Irving Berlin's popular "God Bless America." Originally titled "God Blessed America," with a tune borrowed from the Carter Family's "Little Darling, Pal of Mine," Woody captured the grandeur and democratic spirit of the country, but also initially added three radical, anti-capitalist verses that were overlooked for many decades. Just one of the dozens of songs he was composing at the time, he thought little of it and did not record the song until 1944, when he did include one of the radical verses about criticizing "private property."

After meeting at the Forest Theater concert on March 3, 1940, Alan Lomax invited Woody to record some of his songs for the Library of Congress: "I met Alan Lomax and he carried me down to Washington to the Library of Congress where they recorded several hours of questions and answers and all of the songs I could remember on a pint of pretty cheap whiskey." During three days in late March Woody talked and sang, eventually filling seventeen 16-inch aluminum recording discs. As Lomax recalled: "Woody then came to Washington and lived with me for about a month. He slept on the floor, wrapped in his lumber jacket, preferring that to the bed we offered him. He had his dinner standing at the sink, refusing his place at the table. He explained, 'I don't want to get softened up. I'm a road man.' ... Woody and I worked together like silk." Besides giving numerous details about his life, he recorded "Talking Dust Bowl Blues," "Pretty Boy Floyd," "Dust Bowl Refugees," and much more. Lomax was so impressed that he invited Woody to appear on his CBS radio program, "American School of the Air," on April 2, when he performed "So Long, It's Been Good to Know You."[21]

Lomax next arranged for a recording session with RCA Victor, a major company, in late April/early May, resulting in Woody's two *Dust Bowl Bal-*

lads 78 rpm albums released in July. "RCA Victor asked me to make an album for them and I said 'You're crazy. But I have a man here who ought to do it,'" Lomax would explain. "And so Woody then cut the 'Dust Bowl Ballads' and that was the second commercial folk song album," following Lead Belly's Musicraft album *Negro Sinful Tunes*. Although the albums received scant public notice, Woody had made the big time. Lomax would long remain another of his champions as Woody's career accelerated.[22]

Woody had a magnetic, creative, charming personality that easily attracted devoted friends, although his prickly mannerisms made it difficult for many to remain close to him for too long. Besides recording for RCA, he began appearing on numerous radio shows, such as Norman Corwin's CBS series *Pursuit of Happiness,* along with Lomax's educational morning show, "American School of the Air," his new evening CBS broadcast. "Back Where I Come From," as well as Henrietta Yurchenco's folk show on WNYC, the city's publicly owned station. One evening in 1940, there "was much hubbub in Studio D, guests and performers talking among themselves," Yurchenco recalled. "Someone touched me on the shoulder. 'See that little guy over there, in Levis and a plaid shirt, the one with the wiry-looking hair? That's Woody Guthrie.' I looked around. I had heard about the Oklahoma singer, but had never met him." She asked him to sing "Tom Joad," which he did. "Woody sang the long ballad from beginning to end. The silence in the room deepened, and as he sang the sad tale of the dispossessed people of the Dust Bowl, we all knew that Woody was singing the truth.... We also sensed that he had the quality of greatness." He would often appear on Yurchenco's show. "He represents, better than anyone else, the human unity of rural and urban America."[23]

"His politics, his opinions about life were his own; no one told him what or how to sing," Yurchenco, a longtime friend, would later explain. "He never proselytized but wrote from the heart, from experience, from life itself—and did it with humor and a writer's skill. The irony was that he didn't trust us. We were too intellectual, too eastern, too big-city.... Being with Woody was like walking on glass; we always had to watch out for splinters. Although we admired his songs and integrity, it was difficult to be an intimate friend." Pete Seeger described Woody as "a little bit of a fella" but "he always stood very straight. Not stiff, you know, but straight and relaxed at the same time. He looked sort of the way he wrote. His writing is relaxed and laconic, informal and graceful. That's how he looked. He *stood* in a laconic way. And he was very graceful when he moved."[24]

Along with Lomax and Seeger, Woody began collecting songs for a proposed collection, "Hard-Hitting Songs for Hard-Hit People," although it would not be published until the 1960s. "Here's a book of songs that's going to last a mighty long time," he wrote in the Introduction, "because these are the kind of songs that folks make up when they're a-singing about their hard luck, and hard luck is one thing that you sing louder about than you do about boots and saddles, or moons on the river, or cigarettes a shining in the dark." He then launched into a discussion of his recent rambles. The book included not only many songs by Woody, but also Aunt Molly Jackson, John Handcox, Joe Hill, Sarah Ogan Gunning, various recorded blues singers such as Big Bill Broonzy and Blind Lemon Jefferson, and field recordings by John and Alan Lomax, for which Woody wrote all of the notes. "The songs in this book come from everywhere, just like I did," he concluded. "Only there was just more and hungrier people. Folks that's really been beat up a lot more than I have by the police and deputies."[25]

In late May of 1940, Woody launched a cross-country road trip with the young Seeger. During their stop with Communist Party activists in Oklahoma City, Woody and Pete penned the catchy song "Union Maid," based on the familiar tune for "Red Wing." As he later wrote: "I met up with Peter Seeger, a long tall string bean kid from up in New England and we worked together putting a book of several hundred songs together. We bought us a Plymouth and drove down through the South and then crossed over into Oklahoma to sing for the Hooversville Camptowners 'Community Camp' on the rim of Oklahoma's worst garbage dump." As for Seeger, he was amazed by Woody's intellectual reach and musical productivity. "I learned the genius of simplicity," Pete would recall. "He didn't try and get fancy, he didn't try to show how clever he was. He had done a lot of thinking, and he read voraciously. I remember the time he got hold of Rabelais and got through it all in one or two days, and in the following weeks you could see him trying some of the same stylistic tricks of piling on adjective after adjective."[26]

During late 1940 Woody kept busy in New York with numerous radio appearances, while he continued to compose songs and spend much time with the captivating songster Lead Belly. He also began performing with Gilbert "Cisco" Houston, whom he had met in Los Angles in 1938. Born in 1918, Cisco had bummed around the country, working and playing his guitar, until meeting Woody. In the fall Woody left Lomax's nighttime show. "I am indeed sorry you're no longer on Back Where I Come From," Lomax told Woody on November 1. "The first program that you failed to appear on just about broke my heart and I don't know yet how I'm going to plan the script without imagining you taking lines." They would, however, remain close friends.[27]

Woody was back in Los Angeles in early 1941, when he wrote to Will Geer and his family: "Old Tobacco Road's still a wheeling and a dealing I see. Glad of it. Tell all of the cast I said howdy." And he added, "I reckon you're still a performing for cause parties." The play closed at the end of

May 1941, when Woody celebrated its importance: "So let's scatter a bale of hay and have a celebration and give good old Tobacco Road a big hand. The dirt farmers and the workers are the champions of the world, and some day we'll bring new life to the rotten, deserted farm houses along the back roads and Tobacco Roads of this country." With Woody seemingly stranded on the West Coast, Alan Lomax, continually concerned about his situation, wrote to a friend in March: "Some day he [Woody] will make a great book or a great man, and I wish I had time to sit down with him and stir the book in progress.... A book that I suggested last year [Hard Hitting Songs for Hard Hit People], edited by Woody and very well edited, did not go. Maybe it wasn't sufficiently down the nose to suit the NYC publisher."[28]

Again destitute, having found little to do in Los Angeles, in May 1941 Woody received a proposal from the Bonneville Power Administration (BPA), a division of the federal Department of the Interior, to write songs for a documentary film about the building of the Grand Coulee Dam on the Columbia River in Oregon. He jumped at the chance. Woody and his family arrived in Portland on May 12 and immediately began one of his most creative periods. "Woody showed up in Portland in a battered new car with broken windows, stained cushions, a blonde wife, three blond children and a guitar," Stephen Kahn, who was writing the film, recalled. Lloyd Hoff, who worked for the BPA, has his own memories: "He had a two-weeks growth of beard on his face and he was chewing an apple. To those of us with sensitive noses, it was obvious that he was badly in need of a bath. He was free and easy in his conversation with everybody and completely uninhibited—but he was diamond sharp." After touring the area, within thirty days Woody had written "Pastures of Plenty," "The Biggest Thing That Man Has Ever Done," "Roll On, Columbia, Roll On" and "Jackhammer Blues," for which he was paid less than $300, although a sizable sum when the average weekly salary was only $25.00, for those who had a job. "While he played songs for the BPA office staff, disrupting work in the process, Woody preferred to meet with the working people on dams, the docks, the roads and in the bars," according to Kahn, whose film, *The Columbia*, was released in 1948. A few of Woody's songs appeared on the soundtrack.[29]

"Well, I talked to people, I got my job, it was to read some books about the Coulee and Bonneville dams, to walk around up and down the rivers, and to see what I could find to make up songs about," Woody would explain. "I made up twenty-six. They played them over the loud speakers at meetings to sell bonds to carry the high lines from the dams to the little towns." He loved the natural grandeur of the place, the wonders of modern technology, and the thought of cheap electricity for the working poor while powering the factories of the Northwest that would turn to war production. Late in the year Lomax worked to have Woody record the songs, as he wrote in mid-December, after the Japanese attacked Pearl Harbor and the United States had entered World War II: "I have gotten in touch with the people at the Department of the Interior and I think they may decide to pay for the making of a fifteen minute transcription of your songs about the Bonneville Dam. There will be a fee in it for you, of course." Woody did, indeed, record at least a dozen of the songs at the time. "Roll On, Columbia, Roll On" would later become Washington State's official folk song.[30]

Woody returned to New York just after Germany invaded the Soviet Union in June 1941. The Communist Party and its allies now dropped their call for peace and demanded immediate intervention against the Axis war machine, and Woody immediately agreed. President Roosevelt had done all he could to get military aid to Great Britain, but he was not able to get Congress to declare war until December 8, the day after the Japanese attacked the country's Pacific naval base at Pearl Harbor.

In late 1940 Pete Seeger had met Lee Hays, a preacher and labor organizer from Arkansas, along with his roommate Millard Lampell, a writer born in New Jersey. By February 1941 the three had launched the Almanac Singers, a loose collection of musicians devoted to performing original and traditional folk songs, many with a hard political edge. Soon joined by Bess Lomax, sister of Alan, the brothers Butch and Peter Hawes, and others, they performed for various labor and left-wing groups. "There were others who came in and out, most notably Woody Guthrie from Oklahoma," Bess would recall, "whose persona and brilliance and total devotion to getting the world to listen to him none of the rest of us ever could match." Along with Seeger, Hays, and Peter Hawes, Woody quickly recorded two Almanac albums of traditional songs for General Records, *Sod Buster Ballads* and *Deep Sea Chanteys and Whaling Ballads,* then he, Seeger, Hays, Lampell and Butch Hawes hit the road for the West Coast, appearing at labor union rallies along the way.[31]

"We went into union halls, and sang before, during and after the speakers had spoke, and took up a collection to buy gas, oil, and to grease the breezes," Woody would explain their adventures. "We sang Union Maid, Talking Union, I Don't Want Your Millions Mister, Get Thee Behind Me Satan, Union Train a' Comin'.... We rolled on out to Denver, then onto Frisco and sang for five thousand longshoremen at the Harry Bridges Local. We sang for the Ladies Auxiliary. We sang for the farm and factory workers around lower California, and then back to Frisco." The Almanacs had already recorded "Song For Bridges" for Keynote, about the politically radical head of the West Coast International Longshoremen's and Warehousemen's Union, which was a hit with the union's members. Woody and

Pete finally returned to New York and more singing with the Almanacs, now ripe with "songs against Hitlerism and fascism." On October 31 a German U-boat sank the *USS Reuben James,* with the loss of 115 sailors. Woody quickly penned one of his most famous World War II songs, "The Sinking of the Reuben James," with the tag line "What were their names, tell me, what were their names? / Did you have a friend on the good *Reuben James?*"[32]

Late in 1941 Agnes "Sis" Cunningham and her husband, Gordon Friesen, political activists who were fleeing the mounting anticommunist scare in Oklahoma, arrived at Almanac House, now located on 10th Street. Born in 1909 near Watonga, Oklahoma, and raised in a destitute farm family, Sis had nonetheless been able to attend college, then worked at the labor-oriented Commonwealth College in Arkansas and for the New Deal's Works Progress Administration (WPA) in Oklahoma, all the while performing and writing labor songs. She accompanied her lilting voice on her ever-present accordion. Gordon, also born in 1909, in Weatherford, Oklahoma, developed as a writer, and worked for the Oklahoma Writers Project. Both Sis and Gordon had joined the Communist Party in the late 1930s in Oklahoma, which was soon under local political attack. They married in 1941 and quickly moved to New York to avoid persecution.

They met Woody when Sis joined the Almanac Singers. "It was the first time I had ever seen Woody Guthrie," Friesen would later write, "although I had followed his career from Oklahoma and had a deep feeling for him as a fellow Oklahoman and, more important, a fellow dust-bowl refugee. He looked almost exactly like I had pictured him; he just looked like a dust-bowl refugee from Oklahoma: scrawny, underfed, uncut brambly hair, thin-faced, eyes that had learned to stay out of trouble, or at least not push trouble too far." Friesen quickly became another close friend, as he and Woody roamed the city's streets, two uprooted country boys in the big city. "We made up war songs against Hitlerism and fascism homemade and imported," Woody would recall. "We sang songs about our Allies and made up songs to pay honor and tribute to the story of the trade union workers around the world." During the frequent Sunday afternoon musical gatherings at Almanac House, Sis and Gordon would write, "There was Woody, head thrown back (his black, curly hair always seemed in need of cutting), singing 'Worried Man' or the talking blues about the hens upstairs, 'East Texas Red,' and so on."[33]

Living at Almanac House, over the winter Woody began writing his creative autobiography. "It looks like everybody in New York has wrote a book, so I'm writing one," he would explain. "I don't know the name of it, and really don't know what the story is—that's what I've got to figure out after I get it wrote down—I got about 300 pages of double space scrip—and it tells about every place I ever been, folks I knew, places I bummed around." A speed typist, Woody churned out reams of text, while also composing new songs. In January 1942 the Almanacs recorded an album of pro-war songs for Keynote Records, *Dear Mr. President,* which was released in May, although Woody did not perform. While the songs were contributed by the whole group, Woody had a particular hand in writing "Reuben James" and "'Round and 'Round Hitler's Grave." The Almanacs performed the latter on February 14 during Norman Corwin's widely broadcast *This Is War* radio series, which reached an audience of 30 million.[34]

Woody and the Almanacs struggled through the winter, often freezing in their drafty apartment. "Woody was writing absolutely constantly during that period and we were all working with Woody," Bess Lomax recalled. "He was doing the *Bound for Glory* material.... About a tenth of what he actually wrote came out in *Bound for Glory.* He was absolutely unstoppable. He never even crossed anything out." Bad news came a few days after their appearance on *This Is War,* when the local Scripps-Howard *World-Telegram,* in the article "Singers on New Morale Show Also Warbled for Communists," attacked the Almanacs for their prewar peace album *Songs for John Doe,* although it did not include Woody. A similar story, headed "Peace Choir Changes Tune," appeared in the *New York Post.* Radio and other bookings now dried up. Woody did appear in Sophie Maslow's modern folk/dance show *Folksay,* opening in March, where he met his future wife Marjorie Mazia (he would be divorced from Mary in March 1943). About this time he jotted down some well-conceived thoughts: "Music is a tone of voice—a tone of nature, a sound life uses to keep the living alive and call us back many times a day from the brinks of torture and the holes of superstition. Music is in all of the sounds of nature and there never was a sound that was not music."[35]

Always depending on his friends, as the war escalated Woody witnessed their scattering in various directions. Lampell worked with Hays on the script for the June 1942 Town Hall show "Folk Songs on the Firing Line," directed by Nicholas Ray (the future Hollywood film director who had been working with Alan Lomax on his CBS radio shows), which was positively reviewed by Howard Taubman in the *New York Times.* "The program will include folk songs, spirituals and blues, woven together by a dramatic commentary written by Millard Lampell," noted the *Daily Worker,* and featured the impressive lineup of the composer Earl Robinson, the singer Libby Holman, the Almanac Singers, Burl Ives, Guthrie, Lead Belly, Josh White, Brownie McGhee and Sonny Terry, along with a jazz band led by Art Hodes. Robinson had met Woody in 1940 and recalled he was "Immediately riveting and colorful, authenticity stamped his every gesture. The way he unslung his guitar, and his simple, no-nonsense driving rhythms…. His humor, sure and apparently unstudied." About the same time, Bess Lomax and Butch Hawes, who would soon be married, along with two other Almanacs, moved to Detroit to start a branch of the group.[36]

Pete Seeger was inducted into the Army in July, when Woody moved in with Sis and Gordon, now living on Hudson Street, to concentrate on his book. "Sometimes Woody and I would lie on the floor at night with a couple of quart bottles of beer and talk about the inevitable coming of socialism," Gordon would write. "Woody, Sis and Cisco Houston became the new Almanac Singers and got a few bookings and radio appearance…. Several times a week a bunch of our musical friends would come over for a jam session. There was Leadbelly [sic] with his twelve-string guitar, Sonny Terry with his mouth harp, Brownie McGhee with his six-stringer and Sis would play her accordion, all joining in with Woody to sing hard-travelin' songs." Sis and Gordon would also take off for Detroit at year's end. As for Alan Lomax, he would leave the Library of Congress later in the year to join the Office of War Information, where he worked until his induction into the Army in April 1944. In a folksy letter to Woody on July 9, 1942, Lomax had ended: "The last time I saw you I decided that you were about the most ornery and unfriendly character I'd ever met, and I decided to avoid you like Hitler does Stalin. The hatchet is buried now, though, and I'm off to Mississippi" for another of his collecting trips.[37]

In July 1942 Woody and Marjorie Mazia began occasionally living together in New York, while he worked on his "autobiographical novel." He had received a healthy advance from E. P. Dutton of $250, and submitted a completed manuscript in September. *Bound For Glory* was published in March 1943, to generally favorable reviews, about a month after his and Marjorie's daughter, Cathy Ann, was born. A delightful, folksy coming-of-age story, it revealed little of Woody's radical politics, and would become highly influential, remaining in print into the twenty-first century. "It is hard to guess where autobiography leaves off and fiction begins with Woody," the reviewer for *The Daily Oklahoman* perceptively noted. "Most of his story rings pretty true…. But in any case, he has the most amazing flow of words, his memory, or his invention, is inexhaustible, he has the correct sense of drama, and a vein of native poetry." In his review in *The New Yorker,* the literary critic Clifton Fadiman, who had worked with Woody on Lomax's CBS radio show, believed, "Someday people are going to wake up to the fact that Woody Guthrie and the ten thousand songs that leap and tumble off of the strings of his music box are a national possession, like Yellowstone and Yosemite, and part of the best stuff this country has to show the world."[38]

Eager to enter the war against fascism, his chance came in mid-1943, when he accompanied his friend Gilbert "Cisco" Houston and a new acquaintance, the New York law student Vincent "Jim" Longhi, into the Merchant Marine. Woody eagerly now joined the left-wing National Maritime Union (NMU). Founded in 1937 by militant seamen and waterfront workers on the East Coast, led by Communist Party members, the NMU practiced racial integration, rank-and-file activism, and supported worldwide labor struggles. Union meetings were mandatory for the 100,000 members during the war. "I shipped out with my guitar, and two seaman buddies, both good NMU men, Cisco Houston, a guitar player and high tenor singer, and Jimmy Longhi, an Italian boy with as good an anti-fascist head on him as I have ever seen," Woody would write. As for Longhi, he believed, "Neither Woody nor Cisco had to go to war. Woody had four children and could have stayed out of it or gotten a soft job in the army. Cisco was legally blind.... When they asked me ship out with them, I was honored, thrilled, and terrified. I was trapped between two heroes."[39]

They shipped out three times, first on the S.S. *William B. Travis* in June 1943, which was torpedoed off Italy. "Cisco was on board when I got to the ship," Longhi recalled; "Woody was a little late, but it was no wonder, considering what he was carrying. We could barely see him under the load: a seabag over his shoulder, a guitar strapped to his back, a violin case, a mandolin case, a stack of at least ten books, and a portable typewriter, all tied together by a length of clothesline and somehow wrapped around him. 'Hey!' a longshoreman called out, 'looka the walkin' pawnshop!'" Woody became a messman, working in the kitchen, although he seemingly spent as much time singing songs for the crew as cleaning the messroom. His creative, artistic personality took over. "Woody was standing before the menu blackboard, chalk in hand, putting the finishing touches on the most ornately decorated menu imaginable," Longhi recalled. "The dishes, written in a beautiful flowing script, were framed by birds, flowers, mermaids, and black and white children playing together. The dishes themselves were given new names. Beef stew became 'Aunt Jenny's Prizewinning Saturday-night Special' ... At dinner Woody covered the blackboard with new decorations, which again transformed the prosaic menu into irresistible gastronomic poetry. The gunners set the tables." Later he fashioned a fantastic wind machine attached to the starboard rail that fascinated the crew and was designed, according to Woody, to help the convoy go faster.[40]

The three sailors made it back to the United States in October, and Woody moved in with Marjorie in Coney Island (they would marry in November 1945). The three shipped out again in January 1944 on the S.S. *William Floyd*. After a rather uneventful trip, back in New York Woody and Cisco joined the cast of the antifascist radio folk ballad opera *The Martins and the Coys*—with Pete Seeger, Burl Ives, Sonny Terry, Will Geer—the inspiration of Alan and Elizabeth Lomax for the British Broadcast Corporation (BBC) (it was never aired in the United States). In April Woody, upon Seeger's recommendation, visited record producer Moe Asch's studio, where, along with Cisco Houston and Sonny Terry, he recorded 125 songs, mostly his own compositions, but others that were traditional. "Well, Woody I see that you're a spontaneous type of man, that you don't necessarily think things out, set them down on paper, and then correct them," Asch would later report. "Why don't we try just recording whatever you want…. So he sang about his home, he sang about the West, he sang about his trip, and in each song, he made up the words to folk tunes…. There was a deep philosophy in each song—of the rights of man, of brotherhood, of the inner feelings we all want to express ourselves and yet only the poet can express for us."[41]

Asch operated Asch and Disc Records, and while most of the April recordings were not released at the time, some did appear later. "We yelled and whooped and beat and pounded," Woody described the scene. "We tried hilltop and sunny mountain harmonies and wilder yells and whoops of the dead sea deserts, and all of the swampy southland and buggy bottom sounds that we would make." Following these marathon sessions, which included the first recording of "This Land Is Your Land" (although it would not appear on a commercial recording by Woody until 1951), Woody, Cisco, and Jim joined the crew of the *S.S. Sea Porpoise*, which Woody quickly renamed the *Sea Pussy*, carrying three thousand troops for the invasion of France. Woody exhibited his wild, creative behavior, as well as his heroism during submarine attacks, by entertaining the soldiers, black and white. They made it safely to England, but after disembarking the troops the ship struck a mine, leaving it helpless. The three seamen were unharmed, and made it back to the United States in July 1944 from their third and last voyage.[42]

Woody settled in with Majorie and their daughter Cathy Ann in their Mermaid Avenue apartment in Coney Island. His seaman's papers had been taken away, however, because of his radical politics, concluding his life in the merchant marine. Now he was eligible for the draft. In the fall of 1944 he joined a group of performers, including his close friends Cisco Houston and Will Geer, in the Roosevelt Bandwagon, a touring group promoting President Roosevelt's reelection for a fourth term. The Communist Party had been dissolved in May and replaced by the Communist Political Association, which supported the president and the war effort. This was fine with Woody. By year's end he had a fifteen-minute radio show on WNEW in New York, *Ballad Gazette*, which lasted all of twelve weeks. He also had a few songwriting jobs, including the songs for Sophie Maslow's ballet *Folksay*. In March and again in May 1945, he returned to Moe Asch's studio and recorded over a dozen songs, some traditional—

"Get Along Little Dogies," "Old Joe Clark," "Rye Whiskey"—and others of his own composition—"Woody's Blues," "Ludlow Massacre," and "1913 Massacre." The latter were included on the Asch album *Struggle: American Documentary.*

Having lost his military deferment, Woody received his draft notice in March 1945, just as the war was about over in Europe. Why the military would want a thirty-three-year-old father of four is rather strange, but he passed the physical and was inducted on May 7, the day Germany surrendered. He spent his basic training at Sheppard Field in Texas, then transferred to Scott Field in Illinois to become a teletype operator. Meanwhile, his cousin Jack Guthrie had recorded Woody's "Oklahoma Hills" for Capitol Records, which became a hit. While Japan surrendered in August, Woody remained stuck in the military, although during a furlough in November he and Marjorie were married in New York. He was finally released from active duty on December 21, and formally discharged a month later. He returned to New York and looked forward to his new life, whatever that might mean.

CHAPTER 2

THE POSTWAR YEARS

"Every folk song that I know tells how to fix something in this world to make it better, tells what is wrong with it, and what we've got to do to fix it better. If the song does not do this, then it is no more of a folk song than I am a movie scout."

—Woody Guthrie

Woody Guthrie, Pete Seeger, and their friends greeted the coming post-war world with a general feeling of relief and optimism, yet tinged with anxiety. With fascism defeated, there now appeared the chance to return to their progressive political agenda: supporting labor unions, fighting racism and promoting civil rights, advocating world peace, and the myriad other small issues, such as raising wages (which had been essentially frozen during the war), controlling housing prices, and the like. They also believed that music could play a role in these efforts. On December 31, 1945, Seeger invited a group of friends to his in-laws' house in Greenwich Village to launch a new organization, to be called People's Songs. The gathering included Lee Hays, Alan Lomax, Lead Belly, and numerous others. "The reason for People's Songs is to shoot your union the kind of a song or songs when you want it and fast," Woody explained. "To help you to make a songbook, a program, a throwaway songsheet, a whole evening. … Unless we do hear the work songs, war songs, and love songs, dance songs of all the people everywhere we are most apt to lose the peace and this world along with it." Woody became one of the original thirty-three members of the advisory committee, but soon was elevated to the smaller national board of directors.[1]

Although Woody had recorded a number of albums and published his fanciful autobiography *Bound For Glory* in 1943, following the war he lived in relative obscurity with his wife Marjorie and Cathy Ann. Not that folk music was particularly unpopular. But it could not compete with such popular singers as Frank Sinatra, Bing Crosby, Nat "King" Cole, Peggy Lee, Perry Como, or country-western star Gene Autry. But Burl Ives, Josh White, John Jacob Niles, Richard Dyer-Bennet, Susan Reed, and other popularizers were regularly appearing on concert stages and in night clubs, while also issuing numerous recordings. Alan Lomax kept busy as a record producer for Decca and even hosted his own radio show over the Mutual Network, "Your Ballad Man," playing a range of folk-style recordings.

People's Songs concerts, which often included Woody, received positive reviews. The *Christian Science Monitor* covered a People's Songs hootenanny in Boston in early 1947, noting that "the signs of a newly receptive public have been unmistakable, especially the salable showing of folk musicians on records and their popularity in such places as New York supper clubs." Even Pete Seeger, while mostly appearing at numerous political/musical events, performed at the trendy Village Vanguard night club in Greenwich Village. While Woody remained committed to a radical political agenda, the Republican Party's congressional victories in the fall 1946 elections spelled doom for any progressive agenda, and President Harry Truman, who had succeeded President Roosevelt when he died in April 1945, began to feel pressure to purge any leftists from the government.[2]

As a sign of his unreconstructed politics, Woody returned to writing articles for the Communist Party's press in 1946 and 1947, while quite aware that his political views were becoming increasingly unpopular because of the growing fear of communism at home and abroad. As he wrote to Moe Asch in July 1946: "If your work gets to be labelled [sic] as communist or even as communistic or even as radically leaning in the general direction of boleshevism, then, of course, you are black balled, black listed, chalked up as a revolutionary bomb thrower, and you invite the whole weight of the capitalist machine to be thrown against you." He was most critical of those he felt had sold out to the safe, commercial mainstream. "It is not just a question of you, as an artist, selling out," he continued, "and becoming harmless to the owning side. No, you are never actually bought nor bribed till they have decided that they can use you in one way or another to rob, to deceive, to blind, confuse, to misrepresent, or just to harass, worry, bedevil, and becloud the path of the militant worker on his long hard fight from slavery to freedom."[3]

Woody appeared at numerous People's Songs events, while continuing his prolific output of songs, now many designed for Cathy Ann and her young friends. In early 1946 he recorded twelve songs for Moe Asch's new label, Disc Records, including "Swimmy Swim," "Clean-O," "Put Your Finger in the Air," and "Little Sugar (Little Saka Sugar)." "I really did try to slant these songs at all of your citizens from four to six, but I spilled over a little on every side, because all of us sang and danced these songs and all of us got about the same kick out of them," he would explain. The albums *Songs to Grow On: Nursery Days* and *Songs to Grow On: Work Songs for Nursery Days* were quite a hit among parents and child workers, and would remain among his most popular creations. "My songs are not to be read like a lesson book nor a text, but to be a key to sort of unlock all of the old bars in you that keep the family apart or the school apart," he continued. In her introductory notes for *Songs To Grow On: Nursery Days,* the children's music authority Beatrice Landeck praised "Woody's verses which are full of gusto and vitality. He combines delicious-sounding words with down-to-earth imagery and flavors the whole with humor." His friend, the composer Earl Robinson, would further explain: "The real Woody as I knew him was childlike, inventive, exuberant, brilliant, lovable, manic.... No wonder he wrote such terrific songs for kids. He could observe and penetrate kids' minds, and he knew how to deflate swelled heads." Woody also appeared on the Asch album *Struggle: Asch American Documentary No. 1,*" performing six songs, including "Buffalo Skinners," "Pretty Boy Floyd," and "Union Burying Ground."[4]

In 1947 Asch issued one other Guthrie album on his Disc label, *Ballads from the Dust Bowl,* which included "Pastures of Plenty." By this time Woody's earlier Victor album of dust bowl songs was out of print. Woody urged Asch to reissue it, which he finally did on his new Folkways label in 1950, under the title *Talking Dust Bowl,* including "I'm Blowing Down (This Old Dusty Road)," "Tom Joad," and "So Long (It's Been Good To Know You)"; always in print, this album would be influential in making the songs available to a new audience. According to Guthrie: "I wrote up these eight songs here to try to show you how it is to live under the wild and windy actions of the great duststorms that ride in and out and up and down. That old dustbowl is still there, and that high dirtwind is still there. The government didn't fix that and Congress couldn't put a stop to it. Nobody tried very hard."[5]

In 1947 Asch also published a book of Woody's songs, essays, drawings, and poems, *American Folksong.* It included such gems as "Goin' Down This Road," "Tom Joad," "Jack Hammer John," and "Pastures Of Plenty," although it had limited circulation. "Like thousands of other balladmakers, Woody never pretended to make up everything whole cloth," Seeger explained in a review of *American Folksong;* "he'd take a little of the best of the old, and add something new. He once said, 'Everything I know I learned off the kids.' And it was in the speech of ordinary working people that he found his voice." Asch would remain one of Woody's strongest supporters, but after the children's and dust bowl albums would issue no more for the remainder of the decade. "Alan worked hardest at planning concerts and selling folk music to record companies," Hally Wood, a performer who was married to the radio personality John Henry Faulk and a People's Songs activist, recalled. "Most of us owe him more than we can ever repay. And if it hadn't been for Moe Asch, Woody would have been even poorer than he was."[6]

Woody mostly performed for small People's Songs audiences, although he, Seeger, and Lee Hays appeared before ten thousand striking Westinghouse Electric workers in Pittsburgh in March 1946. He also performed with Seeger, Brownie McGhee, and Sonny Terry, as well as the jazz musician Sidney Bechet, on a CBS radio show, "Hootenanny," in March 1947, based on a script by Alan Lomax. But a month earlier his world had come crashing down when four-year-old Cathy Ann died from severe burns following an accidental house fire. While he would have three more children with Marjorie—Arlo Davy, born in July 1947, Joady Ben in December of the next year, and Nora Lee in January 1950—he would never get over Cathy Ann's tragic death. Yet he could not slow down, and attended the People's Songs national convention in Chicago in November. His feelings about art, commercialism, and politics never wavered: "I think that I have proved that a folk singer, to sing best what the people have thought and are thinking, is forced to turn his back on the bids of Broadway and Hollywood to buy him and his talents out. I feel like my work in this field will someday be seen as the most radical, the most militant, and the most topical of them all." History would essentially prove him right, but for the moment he had little choice as his commercial prospects were slim.[7]

Marjorie's mother, Aliza Greenblatt, shared the Guthries' housing in Coney Island. Woody, from a vague Protestant background who continually devoured new information and different cultures, became very close with his mother-in-law, whom he lovingly described as "a fine Yiddish folk singer and well known poetess." He soon became steeped in Marjorie's eastern European Jewish family background, as well as Jewish history and culture. "She [Aliza] sang Yiddish folk songs and taught Woody Yiddish phrases," Marjorie's friend Irma Bauman would explain. "He adored her, read his poetry to her, listened to her talks about her parents and grandparents, and lapped up her motherly concern." With Marjorie gone much of the time teaching dance, Woody would share child care duties with his mother-in-law who was a celebrated Yiddish poet and active in the local Jewish community. He began writing numerous lyrics about Jewish holidays, such as Hannukah, and Jewish history, although they would not be put to music and recorded until 1998.[8]

His musical output remained high, although most of the political songs did not seem to have much of their earlier intensity and were not recorded. One exception was "Deportees (Plane Wreck at Los Gatos)." In 1948 Woody read a news story about twenty-eight Mexican workers who died in a plane crash near Coalinga, California. They were migrant farm workers who were being sent back to Mexico. Woody had been concerned about farm workers for more than a decade, but now they were Mexican immigrants rather than dust bowl refugees. But they were still anonymous, for the news article mentioned no names: "You won't have a name when you ride the big airplane, / All they will call you will be deportee." He also recorded for Moe Asch an album of songs about the case of Nicola Sacco and Bartolomeo Vanzetti, two Italian anarchists who had been executed in Massachusetts in 1927 for a robbery and killing. This had been a politically charged trial at the time, and remained controversial because many believed that they were framed for their views. The Folkways album *Ballads of Sacco and Vanzetti* did not appear until 1960, however. Woody also composed three songs about a mine disaster in Centralia, Illinois, that killed 111 miners in 1947; the songs were published by People's Songs, but to little notice.

Times were difficult, but Marjorie was working and there were occasional royalty payments. "Arlo Guthrie, 8 wks old, you are sucking your bottle here on my lap good and warm," Woody noted in late August 1947. "And we just cashed our Capitol Songs 'Oklahoma Hills' [the Jack Guthrie recording] for $1155.56 with which we bought today our little red passion wagon.... Bubby [Grandmother] Greenblatt was down good and early already this morning with her postal savings bonds to lend us." Family life had pretty much taken over Woody's days, although he found time for some political engagements, while drifting away from People's Songs events.[9]

The Progressive Party presidential campaign of Henry Wallace in 1948, however, brought Woody back on the road. While the United States and the Soviet Union had cooperated during the war to defeat fascism, by 1948 a Cold War had begun to develop, with increasing political tensions throughout the world. The Communist Party had reached its largest membership during the Depression, then declined because of the 1939 Nazi-Soviet Pact, and became increasingly unpopular after the war with the return of prosperity and the fear of the spread of communism in Europe and elsewhere in the world. The Republicans in Congress had revived investigations of domestic radicalism, while President Harry Truman launched a loyalty program among government workers.

The Progressive Party had been organized in 1947, with former Vice President Henry Wallace as its presidential candidate, and Senator Glen Taylor as his running mate, to promote not only a foreign policy dedicated to peace with the Soviet Union, but also with a strong civil rights, labor union, and economic justice platform. Wallace had strong support from communists and their friends, although President Truman, running for reelection, had a civil rights plank in his platform, which had alienated southern Democrats who now supported the third party segregationist candidate Senator Strom Thurmond. Folk music became an important aspect of the Progressive Party's electoral strategy, with People's Songs organizing musical events throughout the country. Alan Lomax headed the effort, with Pete Seeger and Irwin Silber, executive director of People's Songs, running the music desk. Woody and Cisco Houston performed at Wallace rallies from June to November 1948, although Woody was not pleased with the quality of the campaign's political songs, perhaps except for his own, such as "Wallace-Taylor Train" and "Henry Wallace Man." In any case, Wallace received only a million votes nationwide—compared to Truman's 24,000,000, Republican candidate Thomas Dewey's 22,000,000, and Thurmond's slightly over 1,000,000—and the party quickly faded away.

By the late 1940s, Woody's career was in the doldrums, with scant popular recognition, except among his People's Songs, and its offshoot People's Artists, colleagues. He now appeared in occasional concerts, such as in late May 1949 with Brownie McGhee in New York, and a week later at City College with Pete Seeger and Oscar Brand. On August 26, Woody joined Seeger and the interracial group he had formed, the Good Neighbor Chorus, as well as Betty Sanders and Hope Foye, for a hootenanny at 13 Astor Place; Woody was not the star of the show, just one of the performers. Alan Lomax was always quick to offer assistance, for example, including Woody in a series of short radio "ballad dramas" dealing with the scourge of syphilis. On January 28, 1950, also at Lomax's urging, he joined a crowded stage at Town Hall—along with Sonny Terry and Brownie McGhee, the Weavers, W. C. Handy, Count Basie, and Eubie Blake—in a memorial concert for Lead Belly, who had died the previous month.

Moreover, just at this time there was a quickening of academic interest in his musical life. Nothing extensive just yet, but an inkling of things to come. The folklorist Benjamin Botkin included a summary of Woody's career in his survey of "Folklore, American" for the Encyclopedia Britannica's publication *Ten Eventful Years* in late 1947. The following spring John Greenway, an English professor and folklorist, published an essay on "Woody Guthrie, Modern Minstrel" in *This Trend*, a college literary magazine. Greenway would soon became one of Woody's prime champions. The April-June 1948 issue of the *Journal of American Folklore* included an essay by Charles Seeger, Pete's influential musicologist father, with a brief analysis of Woody's performing style. In reviewing the reissue of two of the Almanac Singers earlier albums, *Sod Buster Ballads* and *Deep Sea Chanteys and Whaling Ballads,* the elder Seeger noted that Woody was "a

man originally of oral traditions who has not reached city-billy" performance style, that is, he had retained a traditional orientation. This was just
a trickle of comments, hardly indicative of the flood of articles, opinions,
and reflections that would follow within a decade or so.[10]

Woody was not surprised by the growing signs of paranoia over communist threats and subversion, foreign and domestic, but one incident was
particularly jarring, known as the "Peekskill riots." On August 27, 1949,
People's Artists, which had replaced People's Songs after its demise earlier
in the year, organized a concert at Peekskill, New York, as a fundraiser
for the Harlem Chapter of the Civil Rights Congress, the civil rights wing
of the Communist Party. Paul Robeson, the popular African American
singer and actor, was the featured performer. A violent, right-wing mob
prevented the concert from occurring, however. A week later, on September 4, a second concert, this one with Robeson and Pete Seeger, guarded by
hundreds of veterans protecting the stage, was allowed to take place. While
not one of the performers, Woody was in the audience and experienced the
horrors that followed, when the audience's cars and buses were attacked
by a rock throwing mob, with many injured, some seriously. Woody was
on a bus with Lee Hays and led the group in singing "I'm worried now but
I won't be worried long!" For the next month he composed almost two
dozen songs about the riot, mostly parodies of country songs, but they
were never recorded. "I remember going through the Peekskill riot with a
gauntlet in the same car with Woody," Hays recalled, "with rocks breaking the windshield. I was literally scared shitless with Woody screaming
at the Fascist pigs who had us surrounded." A week later Woody joined
Pete Seeger and Betty Sanders in a "Songs of Freedom" concert, and at
month's end he was part of "A stone's throw Hootenanny," with the Weavers, Brownie McGhee, and Laura Duncan.[11]

Just as fears of communism increased, which fueled Woody's songwriting output, in 1949 his friends and People's Songs alumni—Pete Seeger, Lee
Hays, Ronnie Gilbert, and Fred Hellerman—were forming a new quartet,
the Weavers. Woody liked to hang around when they were rehearsing in
Pete's Greenwich Village apartment. He had enrolled in Brooklyn College
under the GI bill in early 1950, but this didn't last long, and he was soon
on the road heading west for a few weeks. Meanwhile, the Weavers were
a hit at the Village Vanguard nightclub and secured a recording contract
with Decca Records. They were now backed by the Gordon Jenkins orches-
tra and quickly had hits in 1950 with Lead Belly's "Goodnight, Irene" and
"Tzena, Tzena, Tzena." During the summer Pete asked Woody to rewrite
"So Long, It's Been Good to Know You," for which he received an advance
of $10,000 against royalties, a princely sum that went to his six children,
with Marjorie as his business manager.

Harold Leventhal, the Weavers' manager, had first met Woody in 1947 at a hootenanny in New York, when he was a song plugger for a popular music publisher. "It wasn't until 1950 when I became the personal manager of the Weavers, that I got to know him better and spend more time with him," Leventhal later explained. "In the early fifties, Woody would show up at places the Weavers performed, and I would have to take care of him and get him to his next appointment." Regarding "So Long, It's Been Good to Know You," according to Leventhal, "Woody was at the recording studio in New York when the Weavers recorded his song. He stretched out on the floor and wrote new verses for the song on paper bags.... When Woody was in New York and not drifting out on the road, he would follow the Weavers wherever they performed." Lee Hays had a wonderful memory of Woody and his behavior: "One time he came to the Blue Angel [a nightclub in New York] to hear the Weavers and he wasn't allowed in because he didn't have a necktie. We took him and got a linen napkin and stuffed it around his neck like a cravat of some kind. He stood off in a corner and heard a Weavers' performance." But this was not the end of the story, for after Woody had something to drink "he went off to lie down in Pete's car. At the end of the evening's work, Pete got in the car and drove home, 50 miles up the river [to Beacon], not knowing that Woody was sound asleep in the back seat. He slept until the next day then sat up in the back seat and found himself up in the woods at Pete's house with his cravat still neatly in place."[12]

The Weavers' "So Long" reached number four on the pop charts in early 1951, quickly followed by cover versions from bandleaders Paul Weston and Ralph Marterie. The Weavers also recorded another Woody song, "Taking It Easy," one of their last for Decca in early 1953. Pete Seeger recalled the situation: "Woody was amused by the Weavers. He really didn't approve of us; we got a little too fancy for his tastes. But he came down to the little nightclub we played in, in order to hear us. He was quite pleased when we had a hit with his 'So Long, It's Been Good to Know You.'... There was no mention of dust storms. It wasn't as good as the original version."[13]

It was Woody's most popular song to date, although his cousin Jack's rendering of "Oklahoma Hills" had done well a few years earlier, while the Maddox Brothers and Rose had a country hit with "Philadelphia Lawyer," released on Starday in 1949, which was covered by Tennessee Ernie Ford for Capitol. Woody wrote that the Maddox Brothers and Rose "are the best Hillcountry String band in these 48 states of ours.... I composed a ballad some ten years back by the name of 'The Philadelphia Lawyer,' (The Reno Blues) which I sung for quite a long spell over my KFVD program before I, like all odd folksingers, drifted back to New York City. The Maddox Brothers and Rose made a record of this song on a 4 Star label, and, when the 4

Star man, Don Pierce, took me into his little plywood booth and touched his needle to this 'Philadelphia Lawyer,' my ears wiggled just out of pure, pure joy. I didn't just LIKE the Maddox recording, I fell in love with folklore, folktales, folk poems, folk sayings, and folk of every size, shape, and color all over again. Already, a free sample record of this 'Philadelphia Lawyer' has been sent to each and every radio station in the U.S.A." In early 1952, Decca, thinking of a comeback, recorded Woody performing two songs, "This Land Is Your Land" and "Kissin' On," but decided the quality was too poor for a commercial release. Two years later Moe Asch tried to record Woody one last time in a session with Sonny Terry, Jack Elliott, Brownie McGhee, and Alonzo Scales, but it too was unsatisfactory and never issued.[14]

While his health was increasingly shaky, Woody continued to appear in a concert now and then. Others were not so lucky, as the escalating anticommunist scare began to sidetrack many careers. The Weavers came to a crashing halt by 1953, after they were named as communists in a congressional investigation and by the publication of numerous newspaper accounts of their supposed disloyalty. Pete Seeger was listed as a subversive in the publication *Red Channels: The Report of Communist Influence in Radio and Television* (1950), as was Alan Lomax, who moved to England for much of the remainder of the decade, and Will Geer. Times were tough for folk singers. Lead Belly had died in 1949, while Burl Ives and Josh White had salvaged their careers by cooperating with the congressional investigations. Woody had not been named in *Red Channels* since his career had already been silenced by his developing Huntington's disease, so he was no longer considered a threat to the country. His politics had not cooled, however. "The very first minute that I rize up in body politics high enuff for to pass any kind of a new law and get away with it, I aim and fully intend to pass my law saying it's against the rules of this humanly race here for anybody to sing or talk (or any square mixture of both) for a whole entire afternoon and an evening without protesting, contesting, testing, detesting, and field-testing some of the big and little things you see to be wrong around here amongst all of you nonpolyticklers," he wrote in *Sing Out!* in 1952. "Me, all I know for sure is, you'll always find me over here amongst us protesty ones, the ones, I guess, you'd call the Ticklers."[15]

In the early 1950s, there were increasing fears of domestic subversion from those labeled communists as well as a possible nuclear attack from the Soviet Union. The outbreak of the Korean War in 1950, following the attack on South Korea from the Communist North (the country had been "temporarily" divided at the end of World War II once Japan had been forced to retreat), brought the United States into a hot war as part of the United Nations vote to intervene to defend the South. For three years the bloody battles raged. In 1952 Dwight Eisenhower became the first Republican elected as president since 1928, and his party again took over Congress. The House Un-American Activities Committee (HUAC), the Senate Internal Security Subcommittee (SISS), and Senator Joseph McCarthy's Permanent Subcommittee on Investigations of the Senate Committee on Government Operations, in collaboration with the Federal Bureau of Investigations (FBI), moved into high gear to root out and denounce perceived domestic subversives.

In 1950 McCarthy had begun his claim that the Truman administration was harboring communists, and as he continued to manufacture his charges the headlines grew. He was joined by a wide range of allies, such as Eisenhower's newly elected Vice President, Richard Nixon—who had already launched his attack on assumed subversives as a member of the House of Representatives then the Senate following World War II—veterans organizations, the Chamber of Commerce and other business groups, the Catholic Church, a large variety of conservative national legislators and local officials, the press, liberal Democrats, and so many others. The court trials of various Communist Party officials, along with the convictions of Julius and Ethel Rosenberg for atomic espionage, and the former State Department official Alger Hiss, continued to garner headlines. Thousands of teachers, government officials, labor union members, and others were fired and blacklisted for their real or assumed Communist Party membership or even involvement in communist front organizations in the 1930s, during the war (when the Soviet Union was the country's ally), and after the war. In mid-decade McCarthy lost his position and the Eisenhower administration's fears began to cool somewhat, but it would take a few more years for the Red Scare to substantially lessen, although the Soviet Union would long remain a feared foe. While folk singers were often assumed to be political radicals, and some were, they yet managed to survive through the decade.

Although Woody was little known by the general public, and seemed to be living in obscurity in Coney Island, he was not inactive. The October 1950 issue of *Sing Out!* included his newly written "I've Got To Know," with a strong antiwar message: "Why do these war ships ride on my waters? / Why do these bombs fall down from the skies? / Why do you burn my towns and my cities? / I've got to know, friend, I've got to know." He followed up with a letter to *Sing Out!* in September 1951, as feisty, and political, as ever: "I believe in peace and SING OUT believes in peace; I do my best to fight against war and SING OUT fights just as hard to stop wars as I do.... Let this be the end of those remarks that I will use my Decca contract to fall in love with my bellybutton and forget all of the Peekskills that I've been through with Pete Seeger, Lee Hays, and Earl Robinson, and lots of others." A few months later he reaffirmed his leftwing politics in another essay in *Sing Out!*: "Me, all I know for sure is, you'll always find me over here amongst us protesty ones, the ones, I guess, you'd call the Ticklers."[16]

He might occasionally be seen in Washington Square in Greenwich Village on a Sunday afternoon. "People drifted into the Square from all over the country," Erik Darling, soon to be a member of the Tarriers, and later the Weavers, would recall: "You never knew who might turn up. Harry Belafonte (before he was known), Woody Guthrie, Oscar Brand, and Pete Seeger could show at the square." But at this time Woody functioned pretty much as an image. "The vagabond life was part of the romance that went with the singing of folk songs, at least for big-city kids who had never seen the Depression," Darling would continue. "As inspiration, Woody Guthrie's lifestyle personified this. People drifted in and out of New York, and stayed with whomever they could." It was often difficult to spend much time with Woody. His eccentric personality and sometimes bizarre behavior was exacerbated by his growing alcohol abuse and Huntington's disease. At this distance it is hard to know what behavior was caused by alcohol and what was caused by the devastating disease. Yet he always attracted close friends and admirers due to his folksy ways, keen intellect, and deft songwriting. He kept in touch with Seeger, Will Geer, Millard Lampell, Cisco Houston, Moe Asch, Ed Robbin, Lee Hays, and assorted others, but there were also fresh, young faces, such as Jack Elliott.[17]

Born Elliot Adnopoz in Brooklyn, New York, in 1931, the son of a middle-class doctor, he early had a fascination with cowboys and the American West. As a teenager he picked up the guitar, then discovered Woody's *Struggle* album, borrowed from a friend in high school. The event changed his life, and he soon became Woody's first, most loyal, and most influential acolyte. Having changed his name to Jack Elliott (later known as Ramblin' Jack), he first visited Woody in February 1951, when he was in the hospital following an operation. Elliott followed their first brief encounter with a more lengthy stay in May, as the two played their guitars, swapped songs, and traveled around together. The nineteen-year-old was fascinated by the seemingly ageless Woody (although he was only thirty-nine at the time) and his amazing song and story repertoire. He had soon perfected Woody's musical style, persona, and even some of his idiosyncratic mannerisms. "Some people said I thought I *was* Woody," Jack would say, but "Woody didn't seem to mind." Elliott was fascinated by Woody's ability to spend hours at the typewriter, churning out songs, many new and some revisions of his older tunes, which discouraged the youngster from writing his own. Elliott did not think much of Woody's radical politics, however, but focused on his cowboy songs and folksy persona.[18]

After traveling around the country for a few years, including one trip with Woody to Florida in 1953, Elliott recorded his mentor's "Pretty Boy Floyd" for Elektra before moving to England in 1955, where he became an instant sensation. Dressed in his cowboy boots and hat, never without his guitar, he helped introduce the country to American folk music, and in particular the songs of Woody Guthrie. Alan Lomax was already living in London and promoting American folk singers through their recordings, but Elliott was considered to be the real thing. Lomax connected him with the Workers Music Association, which controlled the Topic Record Company. Elliott recorded the Topic album *Woody Guthrie's Blues* in late 1955, which included "Talking Columbia Blues," "Hard Traveling," "Talking Dust Bowl Blues," and three other songs. The album was well received and not only introduced Elliott to a large British audience, but also made Woody quite widely known, and a major influence on the skiffle fad during the next two years, along with Lead Belly, Big Bill Broonzy, Josh White, and others. Skiffle was a combination of British traditional (New Orleans style) jazz, along with American blues and folk music, played on various acoustic instruments. Elliott's album was positively reviewed in the *Jazz Journal,* while Woody was featured in a 1957 issue of the magazine *Jazz Music,* issued in England, with his photo on the cover: "He could have been a big commercial success (as he is first to admit) but his unspoiled folk purity background and hatred of social, racial and economic abuses wouldn't allow for a double life." While Elliott recorded few other Guthrie songs while in England, although there was the Topic single "Talking Miner Blues"/"Pretty Boy Floyd" in 1956, *Woody Guthrie's Blues* would serve as a monument to both the singer and his muse.[19]

While the faithful Elliott was representing Woody's songs, and even, to some extent, his maverick character, Woody himself was losing control of his life due to his Huntington's affliction. He became increasingly dependent on a variety of friends, including William Stetson Kennedy. Kennedy had worked for the Federal Writers' Project in Florida during the 1930s, and later became a journalist, including infiltrating the Ku Klux Klan (KKK) and reporting on its racist activities, as well a labor organizer. He now lived just south of Jacksonville, Florida, in a sort of artist colony, Beluthahatchee, renamed "Poor Boy Estates." Kennedy had met Woody in New York in the mid-1940s in Alan Lomax's apartment. Their political views had much in common, particularly their loathing of racism. In New York they appeared at various political rallies, and in 1950, when Kennedy ran as a write-in candidate for senator in Florida, he asked Woody to compose some election songs. In November 1951 Woody moved in with Kennedy in Beluthahatchee, and quickly found himself armed with a World War I rifle when the KKK arrived in their pickup trucks, but they were quickly scared off. He was soon back in New York.

Now at loose ends, increasingly drinking and seeming to threaten his children in New York, in May 1952 Woody checked into the Kings County Hospital, suffering from dizzy spells and blackouts. Since his Huntington's was yet undiagnosed, the doctors assumed alcoholism, so three weeks later, after drying out, he was released. But another drinking bout landed him in Bellevue mental hospital in mid-June for a month's stay. He next entered Brooklyn State Hospital for tests, and six weeks later a young doctor finally diagnosed Woody's problem as Huntington's chorea, a degenerative disease for which there was (and is) no cure.

Another old friend, Will Geer, found himself looking after Woody for a while. After living in New York for a few years, Will and Herta Geer had moved back to Los Angeles in 1948, where Geer began a flourishing film career. With Will on the West Coast and Woody mostly staying at home in Coney Island, the two men probably saw little of each other for a few years, as the anti-communist scare heated up in the early 1950s. Geer was listed in *Red Channels* and ordered to testify before the House Un-American Activities Committee on April 11, 1951, in Washington, D.C.; he refused to answer questions about his political past and affiliations. As a result he was quickly blacklisted by the film industry and for some years faced hard times. The Geers sold their Santa Monica home and moved north to the rather remote Topanga Canyon, where, still an avid horticulturalist, which always impressed Woody, he tended his garden and remained aloof from the Hollywood movie colony.

Although Woody was now little known in the United States, he had somewhat of a following in Great Britain within the left-wing folk community. Phonograph records from the United States were very difficult to obtain, including anything by Woody, but Lomax's arrival in 1950 helped to introduce him to a British audience. In early 1952 Woody heard from Ken Lindsay, a jazz and folk enthusiast who worked for the International Bookshop in London, about doing some fresh recordings, or at least releasing older ones in Britain. Woody first responded from Brooklyn, "I think I can talk Moe Asch into seeing the light about giving your firm the rights to release his records." Lindsay encouraged Woody to consider a trip to England. In July Marjorie informed Lindsay that Woody had recently checked himself into the Kings County Hospital, and she encouraged him to continue to write, while she would work with Woody to record perhaps 18 songs. Lindsay next wrote to Woody, "we cannot do with out you in the struggles ahead ... that['s] not just talk ... people like yourself command a great deal of respect throughout the World and altho' the fight is toughest in the States right now, we know that we are on the winning side." Their correspondence continued into 1953, although nothing came of their various plans to work together.[20]

In October 1952, increasingly ill, still thinking he was an alcoholic—his Huntington's was not yet diagnosed—and with the urging of Marjorie, who increasingly feared for the children's safety because of his erratic behavior, Woody moved to Topanga Canyon. As Will Geer would later relate to Ed Robbin, "he came out and stayed with us for a time." This was a one-room stone hut, about a hundred yards from Geer's house. Will and Woody worked together on the garden and various improvements, and the latter soon purchased a steep eight-acre piece of land near the Geer property. In early 1953, however, Woody, increasingly debilitated by Huntington's disease, ran off with Anneke Marshall, the young wife of one of Geer's acting friends, and returned to New York with her. Will and Herta, meanwhile, were hosting hootenannies and plays on their property, mostly with their blacklisted friends, who had formed a local community. In 1953, Will also moved back to New York to renew his stage career, since the blacklist had hardly touched the theater scene. Woody would occasionally visit the Geers at their Greenwich Village apartment.[21]

In March 1953 Woody and Anneke, with Jack Elliott in tow, arrived at "Poor Boy Estates" to visit with Stetson Kennedy, who had already departed for an extended stay in Europe. Elliott soon left, but Woody and Anneke stayed by themselves for another three months. While Woody's commercial song output had long since vanished, he did not stop writing songs as well as letters. Words seemed to pour out of him in a never-ending stream. Songs such as "Pistol Packer" and "Beluthahatchee Blues" referred to the horrors of gun violence and racism, while others mentioned the beauty of the place and his feelings of peace while living there. With Anneke taking care of him, Woody had a restful time until June 10, when his arm accidentally caught fire, causing a painful, crippling burn. A few weeks later they returned to Topanga Canyon in Southern California, where Woody married the pregnant Anneke, shortly after his Mexican divorce from Marjorie in October 1953, then the couple moved to New York late in the year. In mid-September, while still in Topanga, Woody wrote a last, optimistic letter to Ken Lindsay in England: "I'm still whackering out one or two or five or nine of my truefacty balladstory songs every day. Getting more & more classy conscious & lots more testy & protestyius every paussing night."[22]

An increasingly ill Woody attempted to record with Elliott, Sonny Terry, and Brownie McGhee for Folkways Records, but the session proved to be a disaster. About this time John Cohen, an old-time performer, photographer, and friend of Woody, spotted him with Elliott in Washington Square Park on a Sunday afternoon: "Woody was in bad shape, his arm damaged in a Florida kerosene stove fire, his head and beard scraggly, looking like a saint or something that had stepped out of a Picasso blue period painting. A legendary, tragic-heroic figure." Early in 1954 his last child, Lorina Lynn, was born, but the marriage was soon over. Anneke, unable to care for the ailing Woody, filed for divorce in October 1955. Marjorie had already taken over as his caretaker, however.[23]

Increasingly debilitated, Woody still continued to travel, next back to Topanga Canyon with the ever present Jack Elliott, but he soon took off on his own. He somehow managed to make it back to New York and checked into the Brooklyn State Hospital on September 16, 1954. Hospitals would remain his home, with slight breaks, for the rest of his life. He received numerous visitors, including Marjorie and their children, Harold Leventhal, Jack Elliott, and various others. Elliott recorded one Guthrie song, "Pretty Boy Floyd," for the 1955 Elektra compilation album *Badmen and Heroes* before he moved to England.

While Woody had become publicly invisible, there was now a trickle of scholarly and public attention that would become a flood by the next decade. He was not forgotten by his friends on the left. While, oddly, the Weavers recorded only two of his songs, *Sing Out!* magazine, edited by Irwin Silber and published by People's Artists, included his songs in a number of issues, such as "I've Got To Know," "The Biggest Thing That Man Has Ever Done," and "The 1913 Massacre." The November 1951 issue featured "The Great Dust Storm," with this comment: "The songs of Woody Guthrie, particularly the 'Dust Bowl Ballads,' constitute a separate chapter in the democratic heritage of American folk music. Woodrow Wilson Guthrie, from an Oklahoma share-cropper's family, is certainly one of the most gifted and prolific of our country's folk song creators." Perhaps Woody was not from such a poor background, nor was his father a sharecropper, but this bit of fancy certainly fit his persona. A year later *Sing Out!* featured Woody on the cover, and published the words to "Pretty Boy Floyd," plus another short discussion. While the magazine had a limited audience, it attempted to keep his name in circulation.[24]

The scholar and performer John Greenway published *American Folk Songs of Protest* in 1953, the first overview and study of topical songs. While he had written a short piece on Woody a few years earlier, he now devoted a large section of the book explaining his life and songs, with some critical insights. "Like all the composers of the better songs of protest, Guthrie has had a life of almost continuous hardship," Greenway begins his brief biographical essay. "Not all of Guthrie's compositions are songs of overt protest. Of an estimated thousand songs in his manuscript collection, I found only about 140 whose basic theme was one of protest; the remainder fell into conventional folksong categories—love, humor, crime, ballads of disaster, tragedies, and war, non-protest labor songs, and even nursery songs." This was pretty accurate. Greenway quoted from a number of songs, including "Pretty Boy Floyd," "Union

Maid," and "Pastures of Plenty." This was the first scholarly introduction of Woody, and would long remain useful. Two years later, in his survey of *The Story of American Folk Song,* Russell Ames, drawing upon Greenway, concluded: "Woody Guthrie and other singers and composers of remarkable talent like Pete Seeger lead the new generation in adapting the great tradition of American folk song to changed conditions, in the making of original and honest songs."[25]

Greenway and Ames wanted to make a case for Woody's musical relevance in the mid-fifties, but this was not yet possible. The popular Weavers had vanished in 1953, only to return by 1956, but there were others who created a growing audience for folk music by mid-decade. Besides such older performers as Burl Ives, Josh White, and Oscar Brand, there were a number of up and coming artists, in particular Harry Belafonte, The Tarriers, The Easy Riders, and various lesser lights. Belafonte, in particular, had a number of hits beginning with his 1956 album *Calypso,* which topped the charts for over a year, following the success of the "*Mark Twain*" album. At the time, however, folk musicians reached only a limited audience of college students, political progressives, and assorted others who liked songs that dealt with life and death, historical subjects, train wrecks, labor struggles, war and peace, racial issues, and other such real life stories. The popular songs and singers of the mid-fifties, however, mostly dealt with romance and marriage. Male and female singers such as Perry Como, Eddie Fisher, Johnnie Ray, Frankie Laine, Doris Day, Rosemary Clooney, and Teresa Brewer topped the charts until Elvis Presley came along in 1954 to open the door for rock and roll. For the remainder of the decade he led a growing list of performers, including Fats Domino, Little Richard, the Everly Brothers, Chuck Berry, and Bill Haley & His Comets, who all promoted rock and roll. One other, significant difference between folk and pop music was that the latter was designed mostly for dancing (fast or slow), while folk was strictly for listening (and protesting).

A few popular folk performers featured Guthrie's songs in their repertoire. Odetta, just beginning her folk career, and Larry Mohr included two Guthrie-related songs, "I Was Born About 10,000 Years Ago/The Biggest Thing" and "The Car-Car Song," on their 1954 Fantasy album *Odetta and Larry.* The album based on the Weavers' reunion concert in Carnegie Hall in December 1955, released by Vanguard Records, did include "Woody's Rag/900 Miles," their only nod to a Guthrie tune at the time, while their later Vanguard release, *The Weavers On Tour,* featured "So Long (It's Been Good to Know Yuh)," and *The Weavers At Home* started with "This Land Is Your Land." Even Seeger's steady stream of albums for Folkways Records seldom included a Guthrie tune. His 1956 *American Industrial Ballads* featured "Pittsburgh Town," and two years later *American Favorite Bal-*

lads Vol. 2 had "Hard Traveling." The same year's Seeger's *Gazette, Vol. 1* featured "Pretty Boy Floyd," "Roll On Columbia," and "The Sinking of the Reuben James." Moreover, the Gateway Singers recorded a few Guthrie songs, such as "Hard, Ain't It Hard" and "Sinking of the Reuben James." By decade's end, however, even Guthrie's most ardent supporters, such as Seeger, always drawing upon a broad repertoire, found it difficult to perform even a smattering of his tunes. Still, the Kingston Trio included "Hard, Ain't It Hard" in their 1958 block buster inaugural album, *The Kingston Trio,* for Capitol.

Guthrie had essentially disappeared into a hospital ward, but he was not forgotten. When in 1955 children at a summer camp in Missouri wrote to him in the hospital, after hearing the camp music director sing "This Land Is Your Land," *Sing Out!* printed Woody's replies, such as: "I'm sure glad God made me sick enough to make you one and all my pretty angels and send me out such nice letters as yours are." On March 17, 1956, about a thousand gathered for a night of music at The Pythian just off Central Park to honor Woody, who was in the audience, and to raise funds for his family; the night was titled "Bound For Glory." Harold Leventhal and Lou Gordon had organized the event. The audience was shocked to see a wizened, white haired, shaky Woody, looking much older than in his mid-forties. Lee Hays and Earl Robinson were the narrators, working from a script by Millard Lampell. The performers included Pete Seeger, Ed McCurdy, Robin Roberts, the Rev. Gary Davis, and Jimmy Gavin, as well as Marjorie Mazia and her dance group, presenting over two dozen selections, beginning with "Curly Headed Baby," Pretty Boy Floyd," "Vigilante Man," "Bound For Glory," "Union Maid," and ending with the entire company doing "This Land Is Your Land." "As the various artists sang Woody's songs the most surprising thing was that there was not a mood of nostalgia," Irwin Silber explained in *Sing Out!*. "For most of Woody's songs seem as contemporary and meaningful today as when they were first written. If further proof were needed this concert showed that Woody Guthrie has written more of the best songs of our times than anyone else." In May, however, the increasingly ill Woody would be committed to the Greystone Park Psychiatric Hospital in Morris Plains, New Jersey.[26]

A year later Seeger well captured the night, after a photo of Woody appeared on *Sing Out!*'s summer 1957 cover: "But here, in an evening of Woody's songs, we saw the face of America as it was seen by one man, so no matter how widely we circled, we kept returning to a center. Furthermore, none of the singers on the stage did any talking themselves. Millard Lampell had done a deft job of selecting certain paragraphs of Woody's to introduce each number. These were read from the side of the stage by bass-voiced Lee Hays. Therefore Woody's prose flowed into Woody's poetry and then back into Woody's prose without a break." Indeed, Woody's old friend Lampell had done a masterful job.[27]

Since his days in the Almanac Singers, Lampell had led a professionally checkered life. He had survived as a writer in New York until he enlisted in the Army Air Corps on June 8, 1943, and spent most of the war writing scripts for the AAF Radio Network. At war's end he published *The Long Way Home*, an account of wounded veterans in military hospitals, and joined People's Songs, before moving to Hollywood in 1947 to work on film scripts. His career came to a crashing halt when he found he was blacklisted because of his left-wing politics. He moved back to New York in 1949 and struggled through the decade. His listing in *Red Channels* almost destroyed his career, while the FBI continually monitored his activities. Even so, he could not abandon his political views and old friends, and was more than happy to step forward and write the script for the Guthrie night at The Pythian.

A Folkways album, *Bound For Glory*, followed in 1956; it featured the blacklisted actor Will Geer narrating part of Lampell's script between original Guthrie recordings. Will opened with a deft sketch:

> His name is Woodrow Wilson Guthrie—a bit of information which may come as kind of a surprise. Most people don't know he's got any other name but just Woody.
>
> He started out from Oklahoma, and he traveled all of the forty-eight states and most of the seven seas. And wherever he went he made music. He sang and he whistled, he hummed and he hooted, he played the guitar, the mouth harp, the mountain fiddle and the mandolin. If he couldn't lay his hands on a guitar, why he could just bang out a song with a couple of spoons. Or tap out a tune with his bare hands on a tin can.
>
> Nobody does know just how many songs he made up. A collector claims to have counted up over a thousand. But that would just be the ones that Woody took the trouble to write down. It wouldn't include the ones that slipped away in the dusty wind, the ones that vanished in the clank and rattle of a freight train crossing through the hills in the darkness.
>
> All right, let's say he made up a thousand songs. Songs with love in them, songs with loneliness and sorrow in them, songs with a fierce and stubborn will to survive. Some of them, the chances are, you never heard. And some of them were played on every radio station and juke box in the country. And some of them were hummed and whistled and passed along until they became part of the weave of the life of this land. And people would swear to you that they were old folk songs, drifted up through the hickory smoke of history.

Woody's songs have a way of taking hold, because they speak in the voice ofthe people that you can't beat down, you can't scare and you can't starve out. They are songs with the rhythm of work in them, with the echo of anger against poverty and meanness. Songs filled with the determination of a people to damn well endure.

If you are looking for a way to say what the best in America is, you won't find a purer statement than these songs.

The songs included a sampling of his most enduring: "Stagolee," "Little Sack of Sugar," "Ship In the Sky," "Swim Swim Swimmy I Swim," "Vigilante Man," "Do Re Me," "Pastures of Plenty," "Grand Coulee Dam," "This Land Is Your Land," "Talking Fish Blues," "The Sinking of the Reuben James," "Jesus Christ," and "There's a Better World A-Comin'." Geer prefaced each song with a quote from Woody's writings. Since there were very few recordings of Woody's performances currently available—Folkways had only issued *Talking Dust Bowl* and two albums of *Songs To Grow On*—the record was a rare find for his fans. Folkways had limited distribution, however, so buyers had to search out a copy.[28]

The reviews were somewhat mixed, although Jack Elliott was highly impressed: "When I heard this record, I was so thrilled I cried. Strange, though—what brought me to tears was Will Geer's reading not Woody Guthrie singing.... Without having to give an imitation, Will sounds just like what he is. He is a friend of Woody's and understands what Woody has to say." He particularly liked Woody's children's songs, adding "He's got a sort of natural, uninhibited personality—more than any other white man I ever heard—and when he sings into the microphone something of Woody himself gets right on to that tape." John Greenway, always ready to cheer anything dealing with Woody, was somewhat bothered by Geer's narration. It "is a brilliant conception," he acknowledged, but he would have preferred Jack Elliott instead of Geer. He complained to Moe Asch, who responded that Elliott was in England and so Lampell had selected Geer. "Lampell's kindness to Geer, who has suffered more than he deserved in the political stultification of his career, is commendable," Greenway added, "but Lampell's first duty was to Guthrie and Guthrie's material. But as Woody's greatness becomes generally recognized, all of his material will be invaluable, and criticism will become irrelevant."[29]

Two years after the concert, Harold Leventhal, Pete Seeger, and others established The Guthrie Children's Trust Fund to raise money for Marjorie's children Arlo, Jody, and Nora. They published a pamphlet for a cantata (musical show) entitled *California to the New York Island*, including the words and music to many additional Guthrie tunes, and a script again written by Lampell. In "An Introductory Note About the Man and His

Music," Seeger summed up his thoughts about his old friend: "Woodrow Wilson Guthrie, one of the great folk song balladmakers of this century, wrote more than a thousand songs between 1932 and 1952. Some may never be worth singing. Others may stand the test of time, and like 'Auld Lang Syne' or 'Go Tell Aunt Rhody,' become world classics." Then Seeger aptly concluded: "The songs were rarely written to order. Anything worth discussing was worth a song to him.... Though some songs became top sellers on the hit parade, he never composed with the hit parade in mind. In fact, he had a rather disparaging attitude toward Tin Pan Alley and any kind of commercial success. Songs were composed for himself and friends to sing, and he had faith that a good song would get around in spite of the music industry." There was a good sampling of his most known songs, some of which overlapped with the album: "Biggest Thing Man Has Ever Done," "Do Re Mi," "Goin' Down This Old Dusty Road," "Jackhammer John," "John Hardy," "Pastures of Plenty," "Put Your Finger In The Air," "Round and Round Hitler's Grave," "Talking Dust Bowl," "This Land Is Your Land," and "Vigilante Man."[30]

With Woody now unable to talk and with increasing writing problems, Seeger felt compelled to explain and defend his old friend. "Woody was not adverse to having his songs sung on the Hit Parade, but to my knowledge he never wrote a song with the Hit Parade in mind," he explained in the small folk magazine *Caravan* in 1959. "He considered most commercial music men as slick people who didn't really know what folks wanted, but who foisted their own idea of music upon the country." While Woody often wrote and acted in a folksy manner, he had a most inquisitive mind: "Woody had a devouring curiosity. I'll never forget the week he discovered Rabelais, and read through a two-inch thick volume, a relatively unexpurgated edition, in a couple of days.... At the same time he fought to retain his own identity as a representative of Oklahoma and the dustbowl. People thought he was being consciously bohemian, wearing blue jeans in New York, shaving only when it was convenient. But he was just being like Popeye: 'I yam what I yam.'" Woody had deftly mixed his hayseed persona and writing style with cultured mannerisms when necessary.[31]

While few performers included Woody's songs in their albums, John Greenway, a musician as well as an academic, featured four in *Talking Blues,* issued by Folkways in 1958: "Talking Columbia Blues," "Talking Miner," "Talking Sailor," and "Talking Subway." In his liner notes, the album's producer, Kenneth Goldstein, praised Greenway's version of "Talking Dust Bowl," in which he "has done an amazing job of capturing the flavor and mood of Guthrie's performance." Regarding the more obscure "Talking Miner," one of the songs about the Centralia disaster, Goldstein believed that Woody's "close identification with all peoples suffering injustices is so intense, that his songs often take on an air of first-hand knowledge and sympathy which would be difficult to match even by a member of the group to whose defense Guthrie has sprung." Guthrie had already recorded "Talking Sailor," but "Talking Subway" mostly included unpublished verses that Greenway had obtain from the author. Dick Weissman and Pat Foster highlighted a number of Woody's compositions in their similar album *Documentary Talking Blues* (1957), released on the obscure Counterpoint label, such as "Talking Dust Bowl" and "Talking Hitler's Head Off."[32]

While Woody now rarely appeared in public, he would often leave the hospital on weekends. On a Sunday afternoon in late July 1959, Alex Kochanoff was enjoying the folk performers in Washington Square in Greenwich Village, a weekly affair that had begun after World War II: "In the park I saw John Cohen playing the autoharp, so I sat down to listen. I also saw a man drinking root beer and smoking a cigarette. He was accomplishing both of these acts with a great deal of difficulty. A few minutes later I realized that this man was Woody Guthrie." He also had much trouble picking his mandolin. "But Woody is still Woody, unique American poet, who fits his verses to Carter family tunes, and writes songs on subjects which tackled by other people would produce only disgust." This was the first sighting of Woody in Washington Square since 1954.[33]

Woody kept busy with various chores at Greystone, with family visits and other outings keeping him occupied on the weekends. Although long divorced, Marjorie took charge in looking after him, making sure he spent time with his three children. Robert and Sidsel (Sid) Gleason, who lived in East Orange, New Jersey, in 1959 began bringing him to their apartment each weekend, where his children could visit and life could have a normal semblance, until he left Greystone in mid-1961 and moved back to Brooklyn State Hospital. They received packages for Woody and answered his mail. In April 1960 they produced *The Woody Guthrie Newsletter*, with various bits of information about Woody's health and his numerous visitors. "Here it is, March and as we go to press, we're looking forward to more and more opportunities to entertain Woody," they wrote. "We used to love and admire Woody, the folksinger, songwriter, balladeer, novelist, poet. During the past year we have grown more and more to love and admire Woody, the man." He was now, unfortunately, just a ghost of his former self.[34]

The British writer Robert Smith published two articles on Woody in *Melody Maker*, titled "Woody Guthrie today: He put the American story into song," based on his visit to the Gleasons. "Fans come by to talk to Woody, to play a record with Woody, to sing for Woody, or just to tell friends at the next hootenanny, 'I was up to see Woody the other day.'"

He reminded his English audience that Woody's "Folkways and Stinson records have long been considered classics of American folk singing, but only recently, with the awakened interest in folk song and the spate of new records devoted to it, has he begun to gain the recognition he deserves." As for Woody's interest in the current crop of folk groups, "He listens to the Kingston Trio and defends them against purists who resent the melodic changes they practice on traditional material. 'Why not?' he asks, 'as long as its folk music and the folks like it.'"[35]

The folklorist and musician Ralph Rinzler also hosted Woody on Saturdays or Sundays, including the 1959 visit to Washington Square and even a plane ride. Jack Elliott had returned from England in late 1958 for about a year, before traveling back to England (until finally moving back to the U.S. in 1960), and in late August 1959 "surprised Woody by dropping in supposedly out of nowhere. Woody was delighted and he and Jack talked and sang together for hours, reliving old times." Jack would later became a regular at the Gleasons, along with such other Woody friends as Oscar Brand, Pete Seeger, John Cohen, and the performer Peter LaFarge. Woody now had little public image or fame, except among his many friends, but this was about to drastically change.[36]

CHAPTER 3

WOODY'S REDISCOVERY AND DEATH

"Ear Players, folk called them, because they picked up their music and singing without reading the notes, and learnt more and more song everywhere they went, fiddlers that made their violins out of old oil cans, track bow fiddlers, blues and religious players that begged for nickels up and down the street.... Blind and crippled people rattled old tin cups.... Ballad singers of all kinds and colors hit the oil towns ... and there was very little of their kinds of singing that I didn't soak up."

—Woody Guthrie

There was a nothing new about singer-songwriters before Woody Guthrie came along, although the scholarly definition of a folk song was that it had ancient roots with no known author. By the early decades of the twentieth century, however, American folk songs encompassed a large category of not only traditional Anglo-Saxon ballads (i.e., story songs) and African American songs, but also recently composed labor songs, country and cowboy tunes, blues ballads, even nineteenth-century pop tunes, and so much more. Woody's contribution was to be incredibly prolific, composing clever words and phrases while depending on more traditional tunes to get his music across. He was not a professional writer, such as those on Tin Pan Alley in New York who wrote for a commercial market, but also not exactly an amateur. He had not always worked alone, judging from his collaborative work with Pete Seeger, Lee Hays, Millard Lampell, and the other members of the Almanac Singers.

According to Pete Seeger, in a 1965 essay, folk music "is *not* simply a group of old songs. Rather, it is a process, which has been going on for thousands of years, in which ordinary people continually re-create the old music, changing it a little here and there as their lives change. Now that our lives are changing so rapidly, obviously there will be lots of new songs." Woody was definitely a part of this age old process, and would be the prime influence on the new crop of singer-writers just emerging. Moreover, the recording industry had been in flux since 1950 with the introduction of two new formats: the 7" 45 rpm record designed for the growing adolescent interest in pop songs, and the 10" (soon expanded to 12") 33 1/3 long playing (LP) album of classical music and other fringe genres such as folk.[1]

Starting in 1960, with Woody ensconced in the hospital, there was increasing public recognition of his music and image, sparked by the escalating folk music revival. "The folksingers are coming back into their own," *Variety,* the show business paper, announced in February 1958. "With any jazz concerts finding it tough sledding around the country this past fall and winter season, the folksong packages are picking up lots of concert coin." The article focused on Theodore Bikel, Josh White, Pete Seeger, and a few others, but there was little inkling of what was soon to come with the emergence of the Kingston Trio within a few months. Bob Shane, Dave Guard, and Nick Reynolds had formed a trio in 1956 in California, and selected the name Kingston Trio in order to tie into the current calypso fad—Kingston was a reference to the city in Jamaica. Their first album for Capitol Records, released on June 1, 1958, *The Kingston Trio,* included one Guthrie song, "Hard, Ain't It Hard." The album also featured the traditional southern tune "Tom Dooley," which became the number one song in the country by year's end, when the album also received a number one ranking and continued to sell for 114 weeks. Capitol quickly released a second album, *From the Hungry i,* which also became a best seller, followed by the equally popular *Sold Out* and *String Along.* For the next few years they released a stream of popular records, which included a handful of Guthrie tunes—"Hard Travelin'," "Pastures of Plenty," "This Land Is Your Land," and "Reuben James." Their success would soon open the floodgates for folk music's popularity, at least until the mid-1960s, fueled by the buying power of the baby boomers then coming of age.[2]

The jazz musician and club owner George Wein, who had founded the Newport Jazz Festival in 1954, created the Newport Folk Festival in 1959. The next year Robert Shelton, the *New York Times* music reporter, published a loving portrait of Woody in the festival's program, which was later reprinted by the Guthrie Children's Trust Fund. "He is really too short to be a giant," Shelton began. "He's almost too lean and delicate-faced to be a hero. He is terribly ungrammatical for a poet. He's got too flat and inconsequential a voice to be considered a great singer." Despite these seeming drawbacks, "Woodrow Wilson Guthrie is all these things: a giant of a humanist, a hero of the American little man, a poet of major proportions and a singer and composer of some of our greatest songs." Because of his illness he could not be at the festival, but "in many ways, he is here. For he embodies the strongest fibers in the American folk music tradition— the identification with the downtrodden and the reviled, the dislike for sham and pretense, the joy in hearing and making music, the wit, the independence of a man who can't be bought, and the sense of justice that has to speak out or sing out when he sees people being pushed around." This about summed up Woody's importance. Unfortunately, he was not much known in the U.S., while a "majority of the mail Woody receives today is from English admirers" because of Jack Elliott's influence in the United Kingdom. Shelton concluded: "A giant, in the form of a wispy little guitar-picking balladeer, has been among us. He has enriched our music and our literature. He has reminded us about some things easy to forget today, such as integrity and deep-dish honesty to principles."[3]

While Shelton was most interested in Woody's persona and image, others focused more on his songs. Jon Pankake and Paul Nelson, two undergraduates at the University of Minnesota, in March 1960 began publishing *The Little Sandy Review* (*LSR*), a small monthly fanzine dedicated to reviewing recordings while championing traditional folk music and musicians, rather than the commercial variety represented by the Kingston Trio. They planned "to distinguish, in a market of consumer products, those artifacts that were just 'product'—out to make a buck, to entertain, some slickly and some ineptly—from those that had intellectual value, integrity, commitment, emotional depth, meaning," Pankake explained. They also were critical of songs with an overt political message, but they nonetheless revered Woody.[4]

The fifth issue of *LSR* in mid-1960 (the issues were never dated) was fittingly "A Tribute To Woody Guthrie." They included copies of a few of Woody's letters, testimonials by Seeger, the West Coast political songwriter Malvina Reynolds, and the Canadian folklorist Edith Fowke, as well as an extensive discography. In commenting on three albums of Woody's early recordings for Stinson, now available as LPs, the editors concluded: "The listener realizes he is being CONFRONTED with the real and the beautiful in folk art—not the cheap or the easy or the flashy.... This man is a FOLK-SINGER in the truest sense of the word." They even liked Woody's recent Folkways album *Ballads of Sacco and Vanzetti*. Pankake and Nelson had been sending copies of their magazine to Bob and Sidsel Gleason to share with Woody, and they replied: "Woody is quite well. And is very pleased to learn that there are people who remember him."[5]

John Greenway, who had been Woody's prime defender, reported on the declining state of Woody's health in an issue of the *LSR* in late 1960. He pointed out that Woody had been deteriorating for some time and that printing letters by him "will only make him look ridiculous. I hate for this to happen to the one genius of my wide acquaintance, and one of the sweetest persons who ever lived.... [T]o do so would be to do an unforgivable disservice to the reputation of America's greatest folk composer." By this time, however, Woody was unable to write anything.[6]

Woody's songs began to increasingly appear in folk song collections. While living in England, Alan Lomax completed *The Folk Songs of North America,* which was published in the United States in 1960. He included Woody's "Talkin' Blues," "Talkin' Dustbowl Blues," "Hard Travellin'," "Pretty Boy Floyd," "Hard, Ain't It Hard," "Talking Columbia," and "Roll On, Columbia." "The American taste for darn fool ditties and for crazy, surrealist, and rather cynical humour, culminates in the talking blues genre," Lomax explained. "Such songs began to appear on hillbilly recordings in the 'twenties and 'thirties, and it was from them that Woody Guthrie took his inspiration." Lomax had returned from England in 1958 and did visit with Woody.

Early the next year he organized a massive "Folksong '59" concert at Carnegie Hall, with Pete Seeger and his brother MIke, Jimmy Driftwood, Muddy Waters, and the Stony Mountain Boys playing bluegrass. John Cohen, a member of the string-band revival group the New Lost City Ramblers, brought Woody, who recited "Deportee" while Pete Seeger sang it on stage.[7]

Beginning in 1961, short articles and notices on Woody began appearing in various obscure magazines, such as *Country Music Fan Fare. Disc Collector,* published by the International Hillbilly Record Collector's Exchange, included Oscar Brand's portrait of Woody the "Writer." Brand, a noted folksinger, had launched his folk song radio program on New York's public station, WNYC, in 1945 which often hosted Woody, and he was active in People's Songs. "Woody Guthrie is one of the finest writers this country has ever produced," Brand began. "Sometimes he's written verses or paragraphs that seem banal and badly considered. But even these have had the singing quality of poetry and the direct impact of ideas set down in writing by a highly skilled artist. Woody is almost the prototype of the 'American Folk.'"[8]

In the same issue of *Disc Collector* the traditional folk singer Logan English, who had recorded for Folkways, explained that he had not really appreciated Guthrie's songs until he heard Pete Seeger perform "Deportee" at "Folksong '59." "I felt I knew, for the first time, what folk music was all about.... I began to absorb some of his songs and writings," English explained. "At first I was sometimes disappointed that much of his work did not excite me," but not for long. "He forced me to understand the power and strength of song and made me feel the joy of song." English would later issue two albums of Woody's songs.[9]

With so few of Woody's recorded songs available, the widely available Vanguard album *Cisco Houston sings the songs of Woody Guthrie* was welcomed by his increasing audience. Houston recorded the songs early in 1961, two months before he died of cancer, about when the record was released. The album included eighteen songs, such as "Ship in the Sky," "Curly Headed Baby," "Taking It Easy," and "Talking Fishing Blues." In his album notes, Houston aptly characterized his old partner: "Woody has never had any patience with the silly meaningless Tin Pan Alley-type songs that may be sung for a few weeks, vaguely remembered for a few months, and completely forgotten in a year." With some exaggeration, he continued: "People all over our USA and in other parts of the world have been singing Woody's songs for years, and more and more are joining in with each day that passes." After noting Woody's increasing deterioration, Houston praised his friend for confronting "this with the same great courage he has faced everything in his life, and it's been a life filled with more than his share of tragedy." Woody had already written a mutual appreciation of his close friend: "We are lucky, I think, to have a man like Cisco Houston ... singing fighting and militant folk songs of social protest to the honor and to the dignity of the working man and woman everywhere.... This is a big job and it is for big people with big faith in the humanly race everywhere." Robert Shelton's review in the *New York Times* praised Houston's album, which "will indicate why Guthrie is so highly revered." In the same review he commented that the newly released *Ballads of Sacco and Vanzetti* was "not Guthrie at his best. It is so good, though, to hear that small, wispy, nasal, playful voice again."[10]

"Ironically, as Woody's illness deepened, he became the idol of the younger generation, not as a folk hero, but for the way he lived, for his frank language, his disregard for established conventions," his old friend Henrietta Yurchenco would recall. "Even the physical characteristics of his disease—the jerkiness and halting speech—were imitated by his young followers. But in this case they misunderstood him: their idol was sick and they copied the manifestations of his illness." One of these disciples was a young man from Hibbing, Minnesota, Robert Zimmerman.[11]

Robert Zimmerman (later changed to Bob Dylan) was born in Duluth, Minnesota, in 1941, but his middle-class Jewish parents soon moved to Hibbing, a thriving iron range town. Here Bob grew up listening to country music, the blues, as well as rock and roll, and he began to play the electric guitar and the piano. He joined The Golden Chords, a band that idolized Little Richard, Elvis Presley, Bill Haley and the Comets, then moved into other local groups. While music was a mainstay of his life—he also liked Buddy Holly and the bluesmen Muddy Waters and Jimmy Reed, as well as Lead Belly—he brought a motorcycle and adopted an outlaw persona before entering the University of Minnesota in Minneapolis in 1959.

Dylan soon began to devote his life to music, with little thought of being a student, when he met the local folk establishment, particularly *Little Sandy Review* editors Jon Pankake and Paul Nelson. He borrowed their Woody Guthrie records and a copy of *Bound For Glory*. Dylan was hooked. He quickly learned Woody's songs and took on as much of his persona as he could conjecture from reading his story. Dylan just happened to land in the middle of one of the few groups of young Woody experts in the country, and it would be a major influence on the rest of his musical life. Growing increasingly restless, he arrived in New York in January 1961 and soon after went to meet the fragile Guthrie. The family now lived in the Howard Beach section of Queens, but Woody remained in the hospital. On January 29, Dylan arrived at the Gleasons and met Woody for the first time. Soon after, he sent a postcard to friends in Minneapolis: "I know him and met him and saw him and sang to him. I know Woody—God damn." He quickly wrote "Song to Woody," borrowing the tune from Woody's "1913 Massacre," which would appear on his first album, *Bob Dylan,* for Columbia Records. In their review of the album in *The LIttle Sandy Review,* Pankake and Nelson explain that while Dylan borrowed much from Jack Elliott and Jesse Fuller, "Woody is clearly the biggest" influence. "From him, Dylan seems to have taken not only his style, but his whole philosophy of folksinging and songwriting, and, quite possibly, of life itself.... Yet, Dylan is no boring imitator: he has made this style his own, lived with it breathed it mixed it with outside influences and personal idiosyncrasies, and molded it into something that sounds like both Woody's and his own." As for "Song To Woody," they believed it "is a fine and respectful, not cliche-bound, tribute to Woody that is quite moving, and boasts an elegant first verse."[12]

"I had tried to visit Woody regularly, but now it was getting harder to do," Dylan recounted in his autobiography, *Chronicles: Volume One,* perhaps with some exaggeration. "Woody had been confined to Greystone Hospital in Morristown, New Jersey, and I would usually take the bus there from the Port Authority terminal, make the hour-and-a-half ride and then walk the rest of the half mile up the hill to the hospital.... Usually I'd play him his songs during the afternoon." It is not clear how often Dylan visited, and while he mentions talking with Woody, by this time his speech was extremely poor. Still, Dylan did spend some time with him, partly at the Gleasons, which was an influential experience. Dylan was now writing his own songs, at first heavily topical, paving the way for the raft of singer-songwriters soon to emerge and who would claim Gurthrie as their muse. "I tried to explain later that I didn't think I was a protest singer, that there'd be a screwup. I didn't think I was protesting anything any more than I thought that Woody Guthrie songs were protesting anything," or so Dylan would argue.[13]

While Dylan was an expert on Woody's songs, he did not much perform them in public (only in private for Woody) or record them (until 1988 in a compilation album, when he did "Pretty Boy Floyd"), but Woody influenced many of this songs. "When I finally met him, he wasn't functioning very well, but I was there more as a servant—I mean, I went there to sing him his songs," Dylan explained in an interview. "I never really talked too much to him. He couldn't talk anyway. He was very jittery. He always liked the songs and he would ask for certain ones. I knew them all. I was like a Woody Guthrie jukebox." Unlike Jack Elliott or Cisco Houston, Dylan did not introduce Woody's work to a wider public, but in taking on his persona he was most influential in spreading his songs and image. The story goes that the Gleasons even gave him one of Woody's suits to wear for his opening night at Gerdes Folk City, the famed Greenwich Village club.[14]

Jack Elliott had been instrumental in representing Woody in England, and he would continue to play that role in the United States after his return in late 1960. While still in England he had recorded the album *Ramblin' Jack Elliott Sings Songs by Woody Guthrie and Jimmie Rodgers* for Columbia Records, which would be released in the United States by Monitor Records in 1962. Soon after he arrived back in the United States, Moe Asch brought him into the studio to record *Songs To Grow by Woody Guthrie;* he had already produced six songs in England for the Columbia EP *Kid Stuff—Rambling Jack Elliott Sings Children's Songs by Woody Guthrie.* The Folkways recording overlapped with the tunes found in Woody's two *Songs To Grow On* albums, "Jig Along Home," "Car Song," "Dance Around," and thirteen more. Henrietta Yurchenco had a positive review in *Sing Out!,* while the highly critical editors of *The Little Sandy Review* were most laudatory: "Woody Guthrie's children's songs are timeless and will live forever. Here they are sung by Jack Elliott, an early disciple of Guthrie's, and a man who has mastered all the stylistic nuances and profundities required to bring them to full life."[15]

Prestige-International released *jack elliott sings the songs of woody guthrie* in 1961, his last strictly Guthrie album, which included many of Woody's hits: "Hard Traveling," "Talking Dust Bowl," "Talking Columbia," and "So Long." John Greenway wrote the liner notes, full of his usual praise: "Any one of Guthrie's songs on this record could be the subject of literary and esthetic analysis, and all would contribute to the establishment of his unique skill." The album received rave reviews. The blues writer and producer Pete Welding, for example, compared the Houston and Elliott albums in *Sing Out!* Both were excellent, but "Elliott's interpretations are far closer in spirit to Guthrie's own than are Cisco's." Authenticity was important for Welding. Pankake and Nelson gave Elliott a glowing review in *The Little Sandy Review:* "This record contains ample evidence that Elliott is no longer a MERE IMITATOR of Guthrie.... The songs here are now Jack's own and he sings them in a wonderful Okie old-timey style that borrows freely from Woody but manages to be a whole lot more Elliott than anything else." They praised his version of "This Land Is Your Land," then ended on a high note regarding the album: "It is an incarnation of the Guthrie vision of America (and Woody is a great symbol, an archetype, of Americanism) merging with a daring understanding, tremendously mature new talent."[16]

Guthrie's most important disciples, Elliott and Dylan, had a fateful meeting at Woody's bedside in early 1961, which would lead to their long relationship. "Whenever I was around Woody in those days, Bob was there," Elliott told Robert Shelton. "Bobby sort of hung back in the shadows, just watching everything, just listening. Bob was shy then, you know. But, right off, I could see that Bob was very much influenced by everything about Woody." Dylan and Elliott quickly became friends, living near each other in Greenwich Village, and often performing together. Suze Rotolo, Dylan's girlfriend and a close observer of the unfolding scene, commented on their relationship: "Jack Elliott was the son of Woody and Bob was the son of Jack—that's what folk said, and in a way it was true.... Bobby looked up to Jack and they bonded early on when folk music was making itself over, heading into the mainstream." Some of their friends thought that Dylan was copying Elliott too much, but he was not bothered. "He's just tryin' to sound like Woody and Cisco [Houston]," Elliott explained. "So naturally he is following in the footsteps of Woody and Cisco, singing their style. And that's what I was trying to do, too."[17]

Along with Dylan, there was an increasing number of up and coming folk singers who were inspired by Guthrie. They were given an important boost by Sis Cunningham and her husband Gordon Friesen, Woody's old colleagues in the Almanac Singers. They had launched the topical songs publication *Broadside,* subtitled "A Handful of Songs about Our Times," in February 1962, with the guidance of Pete Seeger. Topical songs were not new—many older country songs were known as event songs because they dealt with current news items such as train wrecks, floods, and other personal tragedies—but many had no political bite. Woody and the Almanacs were guided from a definite left wing political perspective, however, which Sis and Gordon decided to update and make current. Their first issue included Dylan's sarcastic "Talkin' John Birch Society Blues." "The main inspiration for the founding of *Broadside* was Woody Guthrie," the editors would explain. "So we began *Broadside* for the purpose of providing an outlet for song writers deeply motivated by local struggles rather than aiming at becoming 'stars.'" Friesen would soon highlight the Dylan-Guthrie connection: "Dylan is a disciple of Woody Guthrie, whose best work can be used to illustrate the fact that folkmusic is essentially of a working class character, and furthermore that folksongs are basically 'protest' songs in which the creators present their complaint against unjust social conditions and demand, explicitly or by indirection, an alleviation of these conditions."[18]

Broadside's editors were quickly swamped by submissions from songwriters, old and young, all influenced by Woody, whether they knew it or not, and motivated by the increasing political and social activism of the time. The modern civil rights movement, sparked by the Reverend Martin Luther King in the 1950s, and escalated by the Student Nonviolent Coordinating Committee (SNCC) and other activist organizations, was accelerating in the early 1960s. The student protest movement would quickly follow, along with mounting antiwar activism against the Vietnam war by mid-decade.

An inner group of young activist singer-songwriters soon jelled at *Broadside*, including Dylan, Phil Ochs, Tom Paxton, Len Chandler, and many others, in addition to the older Pete Seeger and Malvina Reynolds. "These modern day writer-performers, however, are anything but academicians," Gordon Friesen noted in 1964. "With few exceptions they heed Wood Guthrie's oft-quoted advice: 'The worst thing that can happen is to cut yourself loose from people. And the best thing is to sort of vaccinate yourself right into the big streams and blood of the people.' Some of the songwriters in *Broadside* spend as much time on picket lines and at civil rights demonstrations as they do performing in coffee houses, night clubs and college auditoriums." Friesen would later comment on these activist musicians: "There was one thing that struck me: their inspiration came through [Pete] Seeger but went back to Guthrie.... They saw something in Guthrie that attracted them and motivated and directed them much more than anything about Pete Seeger. In fact, Pete invented the phrase 'Woody's Children.'"[19]

The Guthrie floodgates were now open, with increasing albums, books, and articles. Oddly, Moe Asch was temporarily reluctant to release much of his large Folkways cache of Guthrie recordings, although in 1962 he issued *Woody Guthrie Sings Folk Songs,* which included Lead Belly, Cisco Houston, Sonny Terry, and Bess Hawes. Stinson Records supplied a large number of LPs in the *American Folksay* series, however, for those eager to hear Woody's voice. They were also originally recorded during the war years, with a similar lineup of Woody, Lead Belly, Pete Seeger, Bess Hawes, Sonny Terry, Cisco Houston, and Josh White.

Woody's writings and songs, long scarce, were now becoming available. Woody's *American Folksong*, originally published by Moe Asch in 1947, reemerged in 1961 as an Oak Publication. It included all the original text and drawings. Two years later, Ludlow Music, which held the copyright to many of Woody's songs, issued the hefty *Woody Guthrie Folk Songs*, full of scores of songs. In his introduction, Pete Seeger remarked, "Now that Woody is in the hospital with a wasting illness, Huntington's Chorea, young people with their guitars and banjoes are singing his songs and making them famous around the world." The book included many of his familiar tunes, but also dozens of obscure compositions that would not become popular.[20]

Dolphin Books reprinted *Bound For Glory* as a 95¢ paperback, for the first time making it accessible. "When his book finally came off the press [in 1943] and they sent Woody a copy," Bess Hawes recalled in her review of the new edition, "my husband [Butch Hawes], who was rooming with Woody at the time, says Woody didn't say much about it. But he kept holding it and turning it up to the title page where it said: *Bound For Glory* by Woody Guthrie. I myself doubt if he ever read it over all the way; he would probably rather have spent the time at the typewriter."[21]

In 1965 Robert Shelton, always ready to promote Guthrie, edited *Born To Win*, a grab bag of his mostly fugitive writings, along with a sampling of his drawings. To make the case for his contemporary relevance, the cover of the paperback included a long subtitle: "Nitty-Gritty Songs and Snatches from the boss Father/Hero of Bob Dylan, Joan Baez, Donovan, The Lovin' Spoonful, The Mamas and the Papas and Everyone else in the Mainstream of Pop Sound today." "We must look beyond the songs to find the full importance of Woody Guthrie," Sheldon expressed in his introduction. "When his songs, poems, and essays are studied in our American literature classes, this omission may be righted.... He is a wispy-haired, small-framed giant who appeared on the face of the American landscape, spreading hope and belief and a faith in the American democratic spirit." The reviews were mixed. Jack Elliott was laudatory: "There are laughs and grim jokes and some very sad parts. As some of Woody's songs have been sung and recorded by 'pop' groups or "fop' groups and have been 'bitched-up' in the interpretation or 'rendering,' so it is timely to release a bit of the Real Woody for publication." Michael Beardslee, in the Bay Area's *Rag Baby* publication, was critical of this mixed-bag. "The bad stuff sorts out to four kinds," he begins. "There is derivative poetizing.... There is *Daily Worker* rhetoric.... There is the patent American mixture of optimism ... and blowsy self-pity.... And there is the junk every writer piles up." Still, "there are patches of the real thing in *Born to Win*. Guthrie's songs are certain to remain unrivalled [sic] by his other writing." Few could be totally critical of Woody's writings.[22]

With the increasing popularity of folk music, Woody's fame and influence accelerated. "Guitar atwangle, eyes aimed into a far corner, the voice pitched in a keening wail, the singer holds the rapt attention of the shaggy boys, girls and dogs scattered around his Greenwich Village parade," *Time* sarcastically described the new musical fad in early 1962. "In a campus dormitory in Ohio, in a café along San Francisco's North Beach, in a living room in upper-class Grosse Pointe, Mich., other singers with guitars chant tales of tragic love. In fact, all over the U.S. people of all descriptions—young and middle-aged, students, doctors, lawyers, farmers, cops—are plucking guitars and moaning folk songs happily discovering that they can amuse both themselves and their friends." A year later, in April 1963, folk hit the big time with the debut of the prime time *Hootenanny* TV show on ABC, which would appear for about a year. The term "hootenanny," which Woody and Pete Seeger had discovered during their stay in Seattle in 1941, now ubiquitous as a term for a folk music concert, would be used to sell pinball machines, bath jell, Halloween costumes, candy bars, paper dolls, scores of music albums, one Hollywood movie, and just about anything else.[23]

Articles on Woody appeared in publications large and small. Studs Terkel, the Chicago radio personality and author, wrote "Woody Guthrie: Last of the Great Balladeers" for the men's magazine *Climax* in late 1961. Terkel had met Woody twenty years earlier and always remained his champion. In early 1963 Pete Seeger publicized "Six New Songs By Woody Guthrie" in *Sing Out!* "Back in 1951, when the Weavers put 'So Long, It's Been Good To Know You' on the Hit Parade, a Broadway publisher asked Woody Guthrie if he had some more songs," Seeger explained. "Woody replied more or less, to the effect that sure, he had lots of 'em, and by God he'd like to find a publisher who'd publish 'em and collect some money for them, too.... The publisher gave Woody a tape machine, and then the flood began." The recordings were never issued, but a number of the songs were eventually transcribed. Seeger "was thunderstruck to find sixty or seventy songs among them that I had never before seen in my life," including "Mail Myself to You" and five others now published. Many others would shortly appear in *Woody Guthrie Folk Songs* (Ludlow Music), but over the next fifty years hundreds more would become known, performed, and circulated.[24]

"For a long time now his voice has been silenced," Alfred Hendricks commented, with no political animus, in the *New York Post* in early 1963. "The man is Woody Guthrie—balladeer, roustabout, folk hero. And he is alive today, though slowly wasting away in a Brooklyn hospital.... There was a time when the singer communicated with thousands of admirers through his widely known songs." The August 1963 issue of the Marxist magazine *Mainstream* was mostly devoted to Guthrie, including selections from his writings. Seeger remarked that "I learned a helluva lot from Woody. As a person, and as a musician. My guess is that different people were able to learn different things from him. The most valuable thing I learnt from Woody was his strong sense of right and wrong, good and bad, his frankness in speaking out, and his strong sense of identification with all the hard-working men and women of this world." The up-and-coming singer-songwriter Phil Ochs had just written "Glory Bound (The Story of Woody Guthrie)"—"Now they sing out his praises on every distant shore/but so few remember what he was fightin' for"—which appeared in his 1964 debut Elektra album *All the News that's Fit to Sing.* In his essay in *Mainstream,* Ochs expressed the view that the "legacy of Woody Guthrie encompasses much more than the thousand songs he put together and the years he spent singing around the country. His legacy is the same as all the great poets of history; that of truth or the search for truth." He continued: "One of the sad aspects of the growing fame of Guthrie and his songs is the lack of understanding by some and the prostitution by others. I have run across some people who seem to consider him solely as a writer of great camp songs. They cannot fathom or don't want to fathom the political significance of a great part of his work."[25]

Josh Dunson, a recent college graduate who worked closely with Sis Cunnnigham and Gordon Friesen on *Broadside,* edited the *Mainstream* Guthrie issue. He then published *Freedom In The Air,* the first study of the current topical songs movement, which naturally had a section on Woody's influence. "Along with his songs Guthrie's life had great appeal for many of the more restless students," Dunson explained. "They felt the need to reject strongly, in some meaningful way, the security their parents held dear. Thousands of students hitchhiked across country, following Guthrie's travels on Route 66, remembering the verses in his 'Hard Traveling.'" But there was more to the story: "Of course, there was an essential difference between Guthrie's wanderings in search of work, and those of the students who were seeking experience and new values."[26]

Dunson tried to capture some of the complexity of understanding Guthrie's contemporary influences, musical and otherwise, which Robert Shelton tackled in a 1964 article, "Guthrie's Heirs," in the *New York Times.* "As to the songs of Guthrie," Shelton noted, "even his admirers find enough diversity in them to make him a subject of frequent discussion and even disagreement. Was he a rebel or reformer, responsible social critic or irresponsible bohemian, the product of his times or of an hereditary disease that many protesters had suffered from, a chronicler of an era or a poetic voice that ranks large in American letters?" There were probably no answers to these questions, which would continue to resonate into the next century.[27]

Ernie Marrs, one of the current crop of singer-songwriters, took issue with the standard view of Woody as a rustic who wrote wonderful ballads about dust bowl migrants. What about Woody's radical politics, he wondered, and "the most invisible Woody Guthrie of all is the uninhibited and often ribald one. He got downright bawdy, gloriously so, and pretty often at that." On the other side of the spectrum, John Greenway, Woody's early champion, now began to change his tune. He still believed "Woody Guthrie will be remembered as the most important person in the history of American folk song"; out of his thousands of songs, "somewhere between 50 and 100 are as good as one can find in all American folk song." This referred to the early Woody, but with "World War II his songs began to nucleate around hate, the poorest emotion for poetry.... After the war, when he settled in New York, his hate became factitious as he wrote to the order of a small group of leftists who had captured him and countless others." He also suggested a link between Huntington's disease and Woody's flagging songwriting abilities.[28]

Greenway's criticisms came partly from his move to the political right in the 1960s based on his growing hatred of the Communist Party, as well as his fear of the current student radicals. His criticisms even spilled over into attacking Dylan in 1966: "Others have been influenced by him [Guthrie], some shamefully. Bobby Dylan, the idol of the unlaved [sic] student Existentialists, never knew Guthrie when his mind was whole but imitated the incoherent, rambling, pseudo-mystical lines of Guthrie's last letters on the edge of his insanity. Somehow Dylan has convinced a few avant-garde critics that on the basis of these synthetic effusions he is America's most promising young poet."[29]

Gordon Friesen quickly responded to Greenway's slurs against Guthrie in *Broadside*. As for his songs after World War II, "it was exactly during this period that Woody wrote his many childrens' songs. If there's anything in these songs except an overwhelming love of human life and humanity even Dr. Greenway wasn't able to find it." Moreover, to "separate Woody Guthrie from his times, to attribute the songs and prose he wrote about them, to the vagaries of a 'rare mental defect,' is no more and no less than an attempt to rob a great American of his greatness. Dr. Greenway pretends he is using his scalpel only to tinker with Woody's brain; actually he is trying to use it to cut out Woody's heart."[30]

Unfortunately, the increasingly incapacitated Woody was unable to respond to his critics, and could hardly appreciate his growing popularity.

There were many others, however, who eagerly came to his defense. The performer Logan English deftly explained that "Woody would serve any cause that he felt would serve humanity and he was above politics in the pure sense of the word. By this I mean that in any political camp there is a hard core of radicals or cynics who serve the 'cause' rather than the people.... This type of thinking may be necessary for organizations and discipline but it is certain death for the artist. Woody remained an artist." English concluded "that we need his kind today, that his work is poetry of the highest order, that this man in a few songs can tell you more about America than all the history books in the land. He had a talent given to few men—the ability to give people who had lost all hope an awareness of their own dignity."[31]

Folkways and Stinson had a monopoly on issuing Woody's recordings until 1964, when RCA Victor stepped into the void with the album *Dust Bowl Ballads: Woody Guthrie*. "It is a singularly bitter piece of irony that in the midst of America's greatest folk music ground swell, one of its consummate and most influential artists, a man largely responsible for the present wide-spread burgeoning of interest in folk songs, spins out his days in a New Jersey sanatorium quietly, valiantly fighting for his life," *Down Beat's* Associate Editor Peter Welding wrote in the album's extensive liner notes. Woody had influenced the current crop of folk performers, even those who were not particularly political. "A true people's poet, Guthrie told his stories, wrote his songs, delivered his social messages in warm, human terms in the simple, direct, unsophisticated language of the people to whom and of whom he sang so feelingly," Welding continued. Among the album's fourteen songs, two had not been previously issued, "Pretty Boy Floyd" and "Dust Bowl Blues."[32]

Also in 1964 Elektra Records produced *Woody Gurthrie: Library of Congress Recordings*, a three-record boxed-set. The three hours of songs and stories were drawn from Alan Lomax's March 1940 interviews, which he explained in his liner notes. The enclosed brochure also included copies of Woody's writings and drawings, along with an essay by Robert Shelton: "Woody Guthrie's train is bound for glory. It's a safe bet that he wants us to come along with him for the ride." For the first time an audience could hear Woody describe his childhood and early life, and explain the settings of his songs. Josh Dunson posted a glowing review in *Broadside*: "Two pictures emerge. One of Western America in the 1930's, of men looking for work, being roughed up by railroad bulls, of square dance and country music. The other is of Woody himself just as if you had him up for dinner, and he talked about himself, sang you his songs, showed you what he had seen, and told you just what he was thinking." About the same time Everest Records issued *Woody Guthrie,* a first-rate selection of songs including

"Gypsy Davy," "More Pretty Girls Than One," "Hard, Ain't It Hard," and "Rangers Command."[33]

"No one with a critical or historical sense will deny the importance of Woodrow Wilson Guthrie in the contemporary folk music 'revival' and even in the broader field of American popular music," the UCLA folklorist D. K. Wilgus opened his somewhat critical review of the *Library of Congress Recordings*, "though anyone who sees him as a major literary figure needs to be bored for the simples." But there was more to the story. "Perhaps one of the aspects of Guthrie's personal tragedy is that he was a folk artist in the romantic sense of the artist as a sport in tradition. As a folk performer he would rank as a minor hillbilly at a time when his style was being phased out of the commercial music industry. He became a folksinger and composer who interpreted the folk to the non-folk, but had little or no effect on folk tradition." As a folklorist, Wilgus focused on country music's historical dimension and importance, which accounted for his critical view of popular music. That is, Woody was of little importance as a traditionalist, although he was influenced by hillbilly and gospel songs. Moreover, "one of the greatest ironies is that Guthrie songs like 'This Land is Your Land' are now performed by the slick musicians whom Guthrie despised and are becoming staples of the 100 percent American programs."[34]

On April 17, 1965, *Sing Out!* magazine brought together a group of Woody's older friends and younger fans for a concert at Town Hall, "Songs of, by, for and to Woody Guthrie." "The stars of the program were really the songs of the most influential folk writer this nation has ever known," Robert Shelton explained in his *New York Times* review. Pete Seeger joined Jack Elliott, Logan English, Sonny Terry, Brownie McGhee, Patrick Sky, Woody's friend Marianne "Jolly" Robinson, as well as his 18-year-old son Arlo. The night highlighted the range of Woody's songs. "So it went—an emotional tribute to a dying man who has yet to receive his full recognition as a writer who belongs with Robert Burns and Walt Whitman in the awesome fraternity of great national poets," Shelton concluded, with high praise. This was not the first evening to honor Woody, and definitely not the last.[35]

While Woody's popularity began to flourish, and his health continued to deteriorate, the commercial folk song revival was on the downswing. The British invasion, led by the Beatles and the Rolling Stones, had changed the face of popular music, joined by the African American singers from Motown in Detroit and Stax in Memphis. There was still a growing number of singer-songwriters often criticizing the war in Vietnam, but others preferred a more personal, introspective approach. They were particularly influenced by Bob Dylan, who had dropped his Guthrie persona. The change for Dylan became clear during the Newport Folk Festival in July 1965, when he plugged in his electric guitar and, backed by some members of the Paul Butterfield Blues Band, launched into a short, and controversial, electric set. Dylan had already used electric instruments in his recordings, having released the semi-electric album *Bringing It All Back Home* the previous March, which featured "Mr. Tambourine Man," "Gates of Eden," and "It's All Over Now Baby Blue." Moreover, the Animals in England and the Byrds in the United States, led by Jim McGuinn, had also recorded folk songs with an electric rock beat, soon to be called folk-rock. But Dylan's Newport appearance, which generated much attention and confusion, seemed to alter the musical landscape. Acoustic folk music would continue to thrive, however, just with less popular recognition.

Woody remained at the Brooklyn State Hospital from 1961 to 1965, when he was moved to the Creedmore State Hospital on Long Island for his remaining two years. He was now too weak to leave the hospital. "Sometimes I would bring people with me because I felt that Woody would be happy just seeing the person—visually," Marjorie would explain. "We would talk with each other about our children, about happenings in the world and Woody would just listen and enjoy the conversation." Other old friends continued to visit, such as Pete Seeger, along with Sonny Terry and Brownie McGhee: "Woody was in a wheelchair. He couldn't walk anymore, so the hospital attendant wheeled him out into a porch where it was warm. Sonny, Brownie, and I played some music for Woody. We did 'Rock Island Line,' with Sonny blowing his harp [harmonica], sending beautiful notes into the air. Woody must have liked what he heard because you could see how much he wanted to be a part of our little group.... We played and sang until it was time to say goodbye."[36]

"Today he has found a great and eager following in England and is the subject of a strong revival in the United States," Jean Heller optimistically but also sadly reported in March 1966. "But for Woody Guthrie, 53, it is the end rather than the beginning. For the past 15 years he has been slowly, helplessly, dying of an hereditary disease called Hungington's Chorea, an affliction that progressively destroys coordination and runs its fatal course in about 25 years."[37]

In April, Stewart Udall, the secretary of the Department of the Interior, presented Woody with the Department's Conservation Service Award for the beauty of his Bonneville Power Administration (BPA) songs. There was much publicity in the national press, and the Department named an electric substation in his honor. "You sang that 'this land belongs to you and me," Udall's letter to Woody read, "and you sang from the heart of America that feels about this land. You have articulated in your songs, the sense of identification that each citizen of our country feels toward this land and the wonders which it holds. You brought to your songs a heart as big as all outdoors and we are fortunate to have music which expresses the love and affection each of us feels, thought we are unable to express it so eloquently toward this land." Marjorie reported that "Woody was able to understand the citation and to show pleasure, but could make no verbal response." Harold Leventhal "called the award a 'great occasion.' It was, he said, 'official recognition of an authentic culture that this country has long denied.'"[38]

Nine related recordings had recently appeared in the Verve/Folkways album *Bonneville Dam & Other Columbia River Songs. Variety* published a tribute page from BMI, the music licensing company, titled "An Influence on America as Strong as Walt Whitman." As for Leventhal, he had long been visiting with Woody, reporting "to him on the progress of his songs.... All during the years of his hospitalization I was able, with Woody's encouragement, to arrange the reissuance of his early recordings and books." Moe Asch, in his liner notes for *Bonneville Dam & Other Columbia River Songs,* commented: "Had he only a little more patience and a little more faith in man, he would have survived and be part of the movements all around us of the fight for the right of man and his expressions. Little did Woody dream that a nation with all its bureaucratic and officious skin would, sooner than expected, honor him both officially … and by popular ovation."[39]

"One day next week they will walk quietly into the Brooklyn Hospital on Clarkson Ave. to bring the framed citation to the thin, bushy-haired man who is a legend," John Cashman began his article "Folk Hero" in the *New York Post* on April 19, 1966. "Woody Guthrie, his wasted body upright in a wheelchair, will see and hear but he won't be able to speak or to move his body.... The rise of folk music in the last decade has carried Guthrie to the point of legend." The article naturally focused on his dust bowl ballads, as well as his singing "for labor unions and for workers in migrant camps," with no mention of his still controversial politics. A much longer article in the *New York Sunday News* expanded on Woody's current plight: "In the midst of America's unprecedented folk music boom, Woody Guthrie, the wandering balladeer, whose songs did so much to popularize git fiddle style harmony, lies shut up in a Brooklyn hospital, waiting for death. And he is virtually unaware of the multimillion-dollar folk music industry his songs helped create." The piece well captured the popular image that would long endure: "He once was an Okie with an itching heel, a blistered foot and a sun-burned thumb. He roamed the land with a guitar slung over his shoulder." [40]

This broad national recognition was certainly surprising considering his long-standing radical image, and for some a little hard to comprehend.

"During this time his fame has flourished far and wide," Gordon Friesen wrote in *Broadside;* "he had become a legendary figure, a 'folk hero' of the tallest stature, while still alive. Much of the resultant public image is quite romanticized; we have joined in creating a Woody Guthrie who is, as it were, one of the chief Gods of American folk mythology." Irwin Silber in *Sing Out!* was more direct: "I didn't appreciate the Secretary of the Interior pinning any kind of medal on Woody—or naming a dam or a power station for him. Not in 1966. Not in the years of the Vietnam War. There's an obscenity built into that scene somehow—a denial of life." The romantic image of Woody would continue to be challenged by those who preferred to highlight a more complex view focused on his radical songs and maverick persona.[41]

An expansive 1969 article in *Northwest Magazine* noted that a "flurry of protests erupted a year ago when it was first announced the substation would be named for the wandering musical spokesman of the downtrodden who used his scarred guitar to sing out against injustice and sham. But it soon subsided when the BPA, backed by Interior Secretary Stewart Udall, stood firm." The concern was not over Woody's past communist connections, but over other issues, such as that the substation should be named after someone local and not a relative unknown such as Guthrie.[42]

Will Geer hosted a "Woody Guthrie Folk-In" at his Topanga Canyon theater on September 3, 1967. "On a rickety stage last used 16 years ago, long time Guthrie intimate Will Geer narrated the legendary folk poet's story assembled from personal reminiscences and Woody's writings," Dorian Keyser noted. "Will's narration served as a framework for the performance of upwards of 30 of Woody's songs" by a group of local singers, including Bess Lomax Hawes. Geer's theatrical career had flourished in New York during the fifties, then in 1961, with the waning of the blacklist, he starred in the feature film *Advise and Consent*; he was one of the first of the blacklisted actors to return to Hollywood. He began appearing in various films and TV shows, most famously *The Waltons* in the 1970s. "I'm not going to say those days of blacklisting were a happy time," he confessed in an interview in 1974.[43]

Moses Asch now decided it was time to issue the Folkways album *Pete Seeger Sings Woody Guthrie,* from recordings originally made in the 1950s. The eleven selections were mostly well known, such as "Deportee," "This Land Is Your Land," and "Clean-O," except for "Miss Pavilichenko." The latter, written during World War II, referred to a female soldier in the Soviet Union who had killed 257 German soldiers and then toured the United States as a hero.

While his fame mounted, Woody's health continued to decline. "The last time I saw Woody was at a visit to the hospital," Harold Leventhal recalled. "I sat on the cot with him, talked to him and took him outside. There really wasn't much I could say, though, other than 'How you doing, Woody?' and 'How are you getting along?' For me it was a very depressing experience because I had to accept that for Woody Guthrie, the end was near." Pete Seeger had a similar experience: "I saw Woody Guthrie alive just one more time. I was with his son Arlo and together we played for Woody one of his favorite songs, 'Hobo's Lullaby.' It was the only song we could have sung that made any sense. Shortly thereafter, Woody Guthrie, himself a weary hobo, left this hard world." Woody died on October 3, 1967.[44]

Leventhal quickly spread the word, to Woody's first wife, Mary, to Pete Seeger, to Will Geer, and "everyone else who knew and loved Woody. By eleven that morning it was announced on the radio that Woody Guthrie had died. Later that afternoon I got a call from Bob Dylan," Leventhal continued. "He had heard about Woody's death and told me that if there should be any kind of memorial, to count him in. After that it hit me. Woody was gone."[45]

CHAPTER 4

WOODY'S LEGACY

"There's several ways of saying what's on your mind. And in states and counties where it ain't any too healthy to talk too loud, speak your mind, or even to vote like you want to, folks have found other ways of getting the word around. One of the mainest ways is by singing. Drop the work 'folk' and just call it real old honest to god American singing. No matter who makes it up, no matter who sings it and who dont, if it talks the lingo of the people, it's a cinch to catch on, and will be sung here and yonder for a long time after you've cashed in your chips."

—Woody Guthrie

"Woody Guthrie, the American folk singer and composer, died yesterday at Creedmore State Hospital, Queens, following a 13-year illness. he was 55 years old," so began the lengthy obituary in the *New York Times* on October 4, 1967. "For Woodrow Wilson Guthrie, his songs, his guitar and his humanism were his life. He was a wispy, raspy-voiced musical spokesman for the downtrodden who used his scarred guitar to sing out against injustice and sham." Following a detailed overview of his life, the article focused on his "profound influence on American folk singing, from the countless youngsters who sing out at Washington Square Park to such well-known performers as Bob Dylan, Tom Paxton, Logan English, Jack Elliott and Phil Ochs." The piece, as usual, did not mention his always controversial radical politics. Similar, although shorter, obituaries appeared in numerous papers around the country, with such titles as "Woody Guthrie Dies of Muscular Illness Wrote Songs, Sang About Poor People," "Folksinger Dies," "A 'Seeker' Seeks No More," "Woody Guthrie, Folk Poet, Dies," "Woody Guthrie Is Dead—Fabled U.S. Folk Singer," "Woody Guthrie, 'A National Possession,'" "His Were Prideful Songs for

Common Folk," and "Woody Guthrie Was a Fighting Man." The *Washington Post* article focused on his being "helpless for years. At the end only his eyelids moved." Before his illness, however, "he had been a traveling man, roaming the country for more than 20 years. He wouldn't give up the road. Even when fame and a chance for big money finally came, he avoided comfort like the plague and kept on wandering." Most important, he "was a poet of the down-trodden, the poor and the lost." The three major TV networks (CBS, NBC, ABC) immediately carried the story of his death. He was cremated, and his family threw the ashes into the Atlantic Ocean off Coney Island.[1]

Marjorie and Woody's three children naturally worried about the hereditary nature of Huntington's disease, which they discussed at a family gathering. Nora tried to assure Joady that they had to live their lives without the fear of carrying the gene hanging over their heads. Arlo, having developed his own musical fame, would later praise his father for having led "not just a joyful life, but an important one as well." In fact, none of Marjorie's children would become afflicted (Cathy Ann had died in a fire in 1947). Of his first wife Mary's three children, however, Gwendolyn and Sue both suffered from Huntington's and died at the age of forty-one (Gwendolyn in 1976, Sue two years later); Bill was killed in a car accident when only twenty-three, and Lorina Lynn, his daughter with Anneke who had been put up for adoption, died in 1973 in a car accident.[2]

While Woody's past was often shrouded in myth and legend, with a romantic tinge, many of his friends, as the Vietnam War raged, took pains to remind the public of his political activism. When Seeger heard the news, while on tour in Japan, he first thought, "Woody will never die, as long as there are people who like to sing his songs." He continued: "it may come as a surprise to some readers to know that the author of *This Land Is Your Land* was in 1940 a columnist for the small [Communist Party] newspaper he euphemistically called *The Sabbath Employee*. It was *The Sunday Worker*. Woody never argued theory much, but he would have poured his fiercest scorn on those who have sucked America into the Vietnam mess." The New American Library paperback 1970 reprinting of *Bound For Glory* included Seeger's memories of his friend, the country's "national folk poet."[3]

Irwin Silber mounted a similar defense of the radical Woody: "You may love Woody's songs. You may identify with his life style. You may dig his poetry and his rambling prose. But you will not understand the real Woody until you understand that he was, in the most fundamental sense a totally-committed, 24-hour revolutionary determined to turn this whole world upside down." This was certainly not the Woody presented in the mainstream press. Even the Old Left had not always accepted him, however, as Silber pointed out in another context: "The puritanical, near-sighted left ... didn't quite know what to make of this strange bemused poet who drank and bummed and chased after women and spoke in syllables dreadful strange. They loved his songs and they sang 'Union Maid' or 'So Long' or 'Roll on Columbia' or 'Pastures of Plenty' ... on picket lines and at parties, summer camps and demonstrations. But they never really accepted the man himself—and many thought that as a singer, he was a pretty good songwriter, and they'd just as soon hear Pete Seeger sing the same songs."[4]

Lee Hays had numerous fond memories of his old friend Woody, but also some confusion as to the meaning of his legacy. "I think of Woody as representing what I consider to be the mother lode of American humor and American thought which is the same mother lode that Mark Twain mined all his life, which is Midwestern Populist humor and thought," he explained. But Woody's influence partly seemed to rely on numerous contemporary musicians: "Bob Dylan, The Beatles, Simon and Garfunkel, Odetta, Arlo Guthrie, Joan Baez, Donovan, Buffy St. Marie, Don McLean, The [Rolling] Stones, The Cream, and countless others have become cult figures among today's young. All of them use their music to cry out against injustice, to whisper of love, to comment on the loneliness and isolation of man, to exhort, to rage against rejection. Not one of them stands alone because they are linked to each other by their songs.... They are also linked to the generations which came before: to Woody Guthrie and Pete Seeger, to Johnny Cash, Leadbelly [sic], Jean Ritchie, Oscar Brand and Bessie Smith." Hays stressed Woody's artistic creativity, much more than his vagabond, footloose image.[5]

Gordon Friesen in *Broadside* also attempted to clear up some of the prevailing misconceptions. "An obituary in an Oklahoma City newspaper said that Woody became famous in the middle of the 1940's when he sang 'in Town Hall in New York' and elsewhere," Friesen explained. "This is untrue. Woody never became widely known until after he was hospitalized and could not enjoy the fruits of his work. He had a certain stubborn integrity, a profound belief in himself, that precluded any compromise with principle for even a little taste of fame." Friesen's emphasis on integrity would be most important to Woody's old friends, as his popular image took on more of a commercial, superficial bent. As for the current crop of singer-songwriters, "It is significant that they dismissed with disdain those who were riding high during the 'folk music' boom of the 50's—the Weavers, the Kingston Trios, the Oscar Brands, and so on—and went straight back to Woody. It was this instinct for the real and the genuine, the rejection of the artificial, which has given the topical song movement its strong vitality, constantly being refreshed as new songwriter/performers come along. It is in this sense that one can say Woody never died, and never will."[6]

Ralph Gleason, the pop music critic for the *San Francisco Chronicle,* had a quite different take on Woody's past and legacy. "Just a short few days before Woody died, Pete Seeger had appeared at the Berkeley Community Theater in a poignant concert filled with reminiscences of Woody and old labor union songs, which left me with an uneasy feeling that it was all irrelevant now, symbols of another era," he began his article "The Strong Songs of Woody Guthrie." He mentioned the earlier work of Seeger, Guthrie, and Lead Belly, who "fathered the folk music cult in this country," but he now felt their political criticism of popular music was out of date. Woody's "influence, it strikes me, is more in the work of those he influenced than in a direct contact of his own with the public, which is not to underestimate it," Gleason continued. "As a preacher, as a teacher, as a teller of tales, he reached many people and among them, some who, in their own turn, reached millions. To move those who move masses is a special gift and he had it.... The topical song, the protest song, the individual statement, all became big business and mass media material in the past dozen years, while Woody Guthrie died inch by inch in a hospital bed. It's ironic, to say the least." Woody's expanding fame and influence were particularly indicated by the growing popularity of "This Land Is Your Land."[7]

While Woody was being presented in various guises to the general public, there was also a growing interest among academic folklorists, led by Richard Reuss. A graduate student at Indiana University, in 1966 he presented a paper at the annual meeting of the American Folklore Society on "Woody Guthrie and His Folk Tradition," which was published in *The Journal of American Folklore* in 1970. "It is ironic that the man who perhaps was the most creative and dynamic folk artist of the past generation is so little known to folklorists," he began. Reuss's detailed, insightful, heavily documented essay explored Woody's complex role as a writer, composer, and performer, rooted in an overview of his life. "He experimented knowingly, far more at any rate than the stereotype of the unspoiled natural genius would suggest, and his search for an identity as a performer paralleled his quest for a meaningful style of expression as a writer," Reuss explained. "Guthrie chose unerringly; his traditional background was by far the strongest reservoir of form and content his talents could draw upon, and it enabled him to reach heights in his work he never would have achieved otherwise."[8]

Reuss, always the careful academic as well as Woody fan, also compiled a lengthy bibliography of articles written by and about Woody. "An enormous amount of mythology has been perpetuated by idolaters and popular writers, friends who desire that Woody get the credit he deserves from the public, and fans who rework old clichés and biographical synopses because of inadequate source material and time to pursue serious research," he pointed out. "Political movements, right and left, have contributed their own stereotypes." Not that Woody did not contribute "his share of 'lemon' material, and certainly more of it reached print than should have. Yes, as a songwriter, he was one of the best of his generation, and in his better writing managed to avoid much of the cliché terminology of the period in which he worked." Reuss had no connection to the Communist Party, indeed had a rather conservative background, which enabled him to understand Woody from a fresh, insightful perspective. "As a political and social philosopher, his work is more uneven," Reuss continued, "but there is much in his words that is important for an understanding of the times in which he lived as well as his own intellectual development."[9]

Reuss presented a generally positive interpretation of Woody, but his view had already been challenged by John Greenway in his obituary in an early 1968 issue of *The Journal of American Folklore*. Greenway had been responsible for much of the early appreciation of Guthrie, but he was now a political conservative who loathed Woody's radical politics and his old friends such as Seeger. Greenway criticized those who had "hammered folksongs into weapons of subversion," and who had "persuaded him [Woody] that bad luck was a byproduct of capitalism. He was a victim of deceit, but he was a willing victim, and he led others into the same entrapment." Still, Greenway concluded that Woody had composed "a handful of magnificent songs—the songs of the Dust Bowl, the songs that children grow on, the songs that schoolchildren of the Pacific Northwest sing about the dams at Bonneville and the Grand Coulee, and the song that all America will sing long beyond our memory, 'This Land Is Your Land.' And since these will endure, their composer will endure, and he will be the man he must have been to write them." Greenway was able to praise and even partially defend his old friend, despite their obvious political differences.[10]

The long awaited *Hard Hitting Songs for Hard-Hit People*, compiled before World War II but not published until 1967, is a rich musical treasury featuring Woody's expressive introduction. Alan Lomax "got together with Woody Guthrie, then only a few years out of the Oklahoma Dust Bowl, to construct the book," Irwin Silber explained. "They organized it into subjects and chapters. If some subject needed a song that wasn't there, Woody wrote one. Or Woody might write one anyway just being inspired by some particular phrase or idea he got from working on the manuscript. But, most of all, Woody wrote introductions and comments for every song in the book." While often overlooked, Woody's informative remarks richly documented his creative talent.[11]

As Woody's popular memory brightened, the musical landscape was undergoing considerable change. In 1968 Simon and Garfunkel, Glen Campbell, Dionne Warrick, the Beatles, Otis Redding, Diana Ross and the Supremes, the Doors, Stevie Wonder, and Aretha Franklin were among the year's top performers—a healthy mix of pop, country, soul, and rock. The next year the Rolling Stones, Sly and the Family Stone, the Archies, the Isley Brothers, the Temptations, Creedence Clearwater Revival, Johnny Cash, and Elvis Pressley topped the charts. There were various pop and rock festivals in 1969, capped by the Woodstock Music and Art Fair in mid-August, which featured Santana, Jefferson Airplane, Joan Baez, the Grateful Dead, Crosby, Stills, Nash and Young, Country Joe and the Fish, and Jimi Hendrix. Arlo Guthrie introduced the family name to many in the gigantic crowd perhaps not familiar with Woody, although he performed none of his father's songs; his recording of "Alice's Restaurant" surely followed in his father's tradition, however.

As for folk music, it "has been evolving dizzily, exploding, exploding into a new state—or arena," Herbert Russcol explained in the magazine *High Fidelity* in late 1968. "Bob Dylan, the Noble Savage of Woodstock, N.Y., started out as piously ethnic as his idol, Woody Guthrie. Then he jumped onto the rolling rock wagon powered by the Beatles, and was booed by outraged cultists.... Nevertheless, something called folk/rock was heard in the land—the beat with a message—even though Dylan, always one step ahead, has ducked back to nonelectric in his latest album *John Wesley Harding*." The author wondered about "the glorious tradition of protest song, the line that leads back to Woody Guthrie, Paul Robeson, Aunt Molly Jackson, Wobbly Joe Hill, to the protest airs of Tom Paine and the American Revolution? Flourishing, but disgruntled … Of the young radicals, only Arlo Guthrie, Woody's twenty-year-old son, seems to have escaped monotony by virtue of a salty humor and a gritty naïf voice." "The times they are a-changing, all that seems certain is that folk will remain a vital fountainhead of the overlapping converging musical stream," Russcol concluded. In this context Woody's flame would continue to burn bright, as he became the touchstone for all discussions of folk music, past and present.[12]

On January 5, 1968, the *New York Times* printed an advertisement for a January 20 event at Carnegie Hall, "A Musical Tribute to Woody Guthrie." A two-part concert would feature the all-star lineup of Judy Collins, Bob Dylan, Arlo Guthrie, Richie Havens, Brownie McGhee and Sonny Terry, Odetta, and Pete Seeger. The script, again written by Millard Lampell, would include quotes from Woody read by another old friend, Will Geer, as well as the left-leaning movie star Robert Ryan, interspersed between his songs. Oddly, Ramblin' Jack Elliott, Woody's most well-known disciple, was not asked to participate. Izzy Young complained to Harold Leventhal, the event's organizer, about this slight, and, after some discussion, he was included. While his performance of "Howdido" and "1913 Massacre" were very well received, Elliott continued to gripe about the initial snub. Phil Ochs, who had written "Glory Bound (The Story of Woody Guthrie)," and was counted among the most creative of Woody's musical children, was also left out. Bitterly disappointed, he wound up only in the audience. "We've encountered mixed reactions to the WOODY GUTHRIE MEMO-RIAL CONCERT stages at Carnegie Hall last month," Gordon Friesen, a strong Ochs supporter, commented in *Broadside*. "There was some feeling that Woody himself might have walked out on the whole proceedings, in the sense that the ESTABLISHMENT, which he had resisted with all his strength while he was able, took him over when he was dead and couldn't do a thing about it." He suggested that a new Woody concert should fea-ture the singer-songwriters Tom Paxton, Mark Spoelstra, Len Chandler, Pat Sky, Ernie Marrs, as well as Ochs.[13]

Somewhat altered from the original advertisement, the concert's final lineup included Collins, Dylan, Elliott, Arlo Guthrie, Havens, Odetta, Paxton, and Seeger. "The legend of Woody Guthrie did not die with the Oklahoma folk poet last October," Robert Shelton explained in the *New York Times*. "It appears instead that the legend—and the reality—of that protean national bard are beginning to take hold as they never quite did in his lifetime." In a rave review, Shelton continued: "Saturday's concerts were kept on a consciously simple, folksy level. But it would be easy to envision a national company of singing actors devoted solely to return-ing to the American people the artistic riches Guthrie drew from them." This was Dylan's eagerly awaited first appearance since his motorcycle accident in August 1966. "Bob Dylan, seemingly unable to avoid dramatic excitement, did three songs in electric rockabilly arrangements of disarm-ing originality with his five-man band," Shelton noted. While the other performers preferred Woody's familiar songs, Dylan included the obscure "Dear Mrs. Roosevelt" that highly praised her husband Franklin in such verses as, "I was a GI in my army camp that day he passed away, / And over my shoulder talkin' I could hear some soldier say / 'This world was lucky to see him born.'" "Musically, the program reflected the growing worldli-ness of the folk movement," Shelton concluded. "Because so many of the younger singers have worked in recent years in neighboring pop styles, this was a diverse display far from the folk monochromes of the past."[14]

In 1968 Ellen Willis reviewed the concert in a new rock magazine, *Chee-tah*. She argued that commercial folk music had reached its peak in 1963 (although 1964 would be more accurate). But according to Willis, "Then the folk thing died. Because Lyndon Johnson sang 'We Shall Overcome'; because Dylan went rock. And most of all we were tired of apologizing for what we were—not oppressed workers, not Southern Negroes, but middle-class kids. When Dylan and the Beatles showed us how to accept our origins without joining the corporation or the country club, we went with them. But at Carnegie Hall last Jan. 20 it was 1963 again." She loved the concert. The cast, sitting on the stage throughout, performed twenty-eight of Woody's songs. As for Dylan, "he achieved just the right balance, giving the people what they had come to hear—his was by far the most memorial performance—while expressing in the most moving way possible his own debt to Guthrie. I had never seen him so straight, so modest … and so warm." The tickets were only $2 to $4.50, "Woody would have, well, you know, wanted it that way." Clive Davis, head of Columbia Records (Dylan's label), recalled that Woody Guthrie "was being honored, but all attention was riveted to the return of the young, mysterious poet who had haunted so many minds"—Dylan.[15]

Eli Jaffe was in the audience at the first Carnegie concert. An old friend of Sis Cunningham and Gordon Friesen, he was one of the Communist Party activists in Oklahoma City who had been persecuted in 1941 for their radicalism and had long respected Woody. Jaffe had first met him in the late 1930s and recalled Woody singing "I'm Goin' Down This Road Feeling Bad." "They buried Woody Guthrie at Carnegie Hall, and it was just the kind of funeral he would have enjoyed—people singing his songs, not shedding their tears," he wrote in *Broadside*. "Woody trod this earth for 55 years and the rich legacy he bequeathed it was dramatically underscored from the moment the entire company came onstage singing, 'this train is bound for glory—this train." Following a brief overview of Woody's life, Jaffe recalled a particular incident in 1940, when he was an organizer for the Workers Alliance in Oklahoma City. Guthrie and Seeger were passing through the city on their cross-country trip and dropped by a meeting to support the Tenant Farmers Union. "Just as it was getting started the hall was invaded by a bunch of 99 and 44/100 percent pure patriotic Legion boys and goons and finks. They were threatening and ugly, bent on starting a fight and busting up the meeting. But when Woody and Pete sang their songs it seemed to soothe the savage breasts. The invaders stood and listened and never got around to doing what they came for. Maybe it was the songs and maybe it was the songs coupled with the determined faces of our union men and union maids." That night Woody and Pete composed "Union Maid," to the tune of the folk song "Red Wing." During the war Jaffe would visit with Woody in New York. "And so, in the final analysis, this musical tribute in Carnegie Hall was a deeply heartfelt thank-you," Jaffe concluded. "So long, Woody, it's been good to know you." His feelings were vastly different from those in the audience there to cheer Dylan, but who had perhaps little knowledge of Guthrie.[16]

The Hollywood Bowl in Los Angles hosted a second tribute celebration on September 12, 1970, with the proceeds also going to the Committee to Combat Huntington's Disease, headed by Marjorie Guthrie. The lineup was roughly similar, now including Joan Baez, Elliott, Arlo Guthrie, Odetta, Country Joe McDonald, Havens, Earl Robinson, and Pete Seeger. Will Geer shared the narration with the actor Peter Fonda, and again all of the songs were Woody's except for Baez singing Goebel Reeves' "Hobo's Lullaby," one of Woody's favorites. "Like most benefit concerts, this one had some awkward moments when performers, hampered by the briefest of rehearsals, didn't know what song to sing next or which microphone to use," Robert Hilburn commented in his review in the *Los Angeles Times.* "The closing 'This Land Is Your Land' was a virtual free-for-all with singers unsure of who was to take the lead vocals. But the song, in its setting, couldn't miss." Hilburn concluded that "Guthrie's work is an important part of this country's musical heritage," and because his songs were standing the test of time, "Saturday's tribute was well deserved."[17]

Two albums from the tribute concerts were issued in 1972, split between Columbia Records and Warner Bros. Records, along with a book, *A Tribute To Woody Guthrie,* which included the lyrics for all twenty-nine of the performed songs. "Nowadays guitar-players and banjo-pickers scramble everywhere like field mice," Lampell wrote in the book's introduction. "A honey-haired girl from Connecticut drives a Mercedes bought with the royalties from her album of mountain sorrows. Funky singing groups fly first-class and are living the simple, rural life on 200-acre spreads in old farmhouses, filled with ninety thousand dollars worth of amplifiers, tape decks and stereo equipment." But it was not always so. "It's not easy to believe that in 1940 when Woody came east to join the Almanacs there weren't but about a dozen country or folk singers who had ventured north of the Blue Ridge Mountains. When a dude pushed into a subway lugging a guitar, people gawked as though he was carrying a kayak. The first time I met Woody was in 1940," when Lampell was living with Lee Hays. "He ambled in, unshaven and flat broke, with his guitar slung across his back. Saying with a dry grin, 'Feel like I been shot at and missed, shit at and hit.'" Over the years they became friends, but not without their differences. "An ornery bastard, irresponsible. He couldn't show up anywhere on time. Couldn't hammer a nail straight. Never knew when to quit drinking. Couldn't cure himself of wandering off, vanishing without a word to anybody, deserting those he cared for most. But beneath his sinewy, matter-of-fact manner there was something lost, lonely and gentle. He had a kid's directness, a kid's vulnerability. A kid's poetry. A kid's craziness. A lot of his best work sprang from the part of him that remained forever six years old.... A little guy sloping down a dusty road, looking for something he couldn't name."[18]

Many of Woody's friend assembled at a party in New York in early 1972 to greet the two albums from the memorial concerts. Pete Seeger and Millard Lampell were swapping Woody stories about their experiences with the Almanac Singers. "We sang Woody's songs all across the country," Seeger recalled. "They were great because he always wrote for the man in the corner bar. But his simplification was as purposeful as that of Thoreau's 'Walden.'" Lampell responded: "I saw a football game on TV the other day and at the half they had little girls dolled up in red-white-and blue bikinis singing 'This Land Is Your Land,'" and Seeger countered, "Now, there's a song sung by two hundred million Americans, most of whom forget that it was written by a guy who called himself a Communist and wrote a column for the *Daily Worker*."[19]

Country Joe McDonald's appearance at the Hollywood Bowl event, singing "Woman At Home," one of Woody's previously unrecorded songs, was no accident. Having grown up in Southern California, in a left-wing family, and steeped in country music as well as rhythm and blues, following his military service he moved to Berkeley in 1965. He plunged into the local musical scene and antiwar movement, and soon wrote "Fixin' to Die Rag," a jaunty, sarcastic peace song (which became a hit at the Woodstock music festival). Within a year McDonald had joined with others to launch Country Joe and the Fish, which became one of the most prominent rock bands in the thriving, psychedelic San Francisco music scene. He never abandoned his life as an acoustic guitar player and disciple of Woody Guthrie, however. In 1969 Vanguard issued his album *Thinking of Woody Guthrie* that featured ten of the bard's mostly well-known songs, plus "When the Curfew Blows," and ending with "This Land is Your Land." Recorded in Nashville, McDonald was backed by an A-list of country session musicians, including Grady Martin on the dobro (a guitar with a built in resonator that was popular in country music bands). While his rock career mostly dominated his musical life, starting in 2001 McDonald began touring the country with a one-man show, mixing Woody's songs and words with memories of his own father's hardscrabble life. "Over the years now I have performed my tribute about a dozen times in England and in the United States," Country Joe explains on his website. "Each time I find something new about Woody and about myself."[20]

Since its founding in 1959, the Newport Folk Festival had not ignored Woody, but in July 1968 it featured a segment in his honor on Sunday night. The eclectic festival attracted 70,000 that year, proof that folk, however defined, was still very much alive. The Guthrie tribute included Jack Elliott, Arlo Guthrie, Pete Seeger, along with Millard Lampell and a few of the remaining Almanac Singers such as Bess Hawes. "I might have enjoyed this more if I had not seen the original Memorial, at Carnegie Hall, which was warmer and better organized, and had Bob Dylan besides," Ellen Willis commented in the *New Yorker*. "Still, it was a good way to end. Guthrie represents the best of what the Newport Folk Festival has stood for; his songs transcend fashion—as all folk music is supposed to do, though little of it does. An hour of "This Train" and "Talkin' Dust Bowl" and "This Land Is Your Land" did a lot to soothe the bitterness of the up-tight weekend." The festival would last one more year in Newport, then vanish until resurrected in 1985. Robert Shelton, one of Woody's prime fans, had covered the 1968 event for the *New York Times*, then moved to England.[21]

The 1972 issue of the two Guthrie tribute concert albums prompted the noted jazz critic Nat Hentoff to title his review "Woody Guthrie Still Prowls Our Memories": "The results are not all incandescent, but in general the performers remain affectionately aware of Woody's intentions; and the songs themselves are grittily, often gloriously, indestructible. Standing out are Dylan, Seeger, Arlo Guthrie and Jack Elliott. The latter, who worked so long to be Woody's mirror image, has grown into himself, thereby making his tribute all the more affecting." Hentoff also covered another 1972 Guthrie tribute album, Vanguard's 2-record release *The Greatest Songs of Woody Guthrie*, composed of only previously released recordings. Woody was here joined by the Weavers, Cisco Houston, Country Joe McDonald, Joan Baez, Odetta, and a few others. "Of most value are the presence of Woody himself and Cisco Houston," Hentoff deftly comments. "No instrumental virtuoso by any means, and a singer of limited range and color, Woody nonetheless was his most compelling interpreter, there being no way to separate the music from the man who mined the American experience so widely and deeply."[22]

Throughout the 1970s and into the 1980s (she died in 1983), Marjorie Guthrie devoted much of her life to promoting Woody's legacy as well as funding Huntington's research. She once said, "When Woody was first placed in the hospital some people told me to just write him off as dead. But I couldn't do that. Woody is part of our family. You don't just write off a member of the family." Since there was yet no biography of Woody, in 1970 she collaborated with their old friend Henrietta Yurchenco in publishing *A Mighty Hard Road: The Woody Guthrie Story*. In her foreword, Yurchenco declared: "It has been my aim in writing this book to tell the story of Woody Guthrie exactly as it happened." Yurchenco had produced Woody on her WNYC folk show in 1940 and had a long personal relationship with him. By this time, however, she had become a scholar and an academic and was a Professor of Music Education at the City University of New York. She had access to much unpublished material then in Marjorie's possession, and filled the book with quotations from Woody as well as photographs and song lyrics. "A generation has passed since Woody sang his first song," Yurchenco wrote, reflecting on Woody's current relevance. "We are again at war; there is poverty in the midst of plenty, and hate among our people where love should be. Again, as in Guthrie's time, society is in ferment. Again, the conscience of youth has been stirred to action, as young people become aware of the threat to the individual in the facelessness of our mechanized world." Although Woody had actually begun writing songs before World War II, Yurchenco correctly connected his sensibilities with the current political upheavals over the war in Vietnam and so many other domestic problems.[23]

Marjorie worked with Harold Leventhal and others to produce *Woody Sez*, published by Grosset & Dunlap in 1975, a compilation of his early articles for the *People's World* along with numerous drawings. "Woodrow Wilson Guthrie was a tough little piece of leather," the Chicago radio personality and popular author Studs Terkel wrote in the book's introduction, "and an even tougher, bigger piece of man.... The funny thing is he never regarded himself as unique. He believed everybody was unique." An expressive spokesman for the common man himself, Terkel well stated, "there is no better chronicle of hard times than Woody's Dust Bowl ballads. Nor are there more eloquent anthems to man's potential than his Columbia Valley songs. And always there was a sense of wonder and astonishment.... At a time of such stunning banality as we now experience, his songs and writings are more than stirring. They are necessary. So is this book." It got some decent publicity, including Barbara Walters leading a discussion about Woody with Pete Seeger and Arlo Guthrie for NBC-TV's *The Today Show* on February 27, 1975.[24]

The following year Marjorie and Leventhal published the hefty *Woody Guthrie Songbook,* with scores of songs and numerous, wonderful illustrations. Will Geer included a short essay of his memories of the "Early Guthrie": "One of the great joys of life is discovering someone that feels and thinks as you do and won't let you keep it bottled up inside. Such a one was Woody. He loved to force you out of hibernation and get you mad enough to spit back." Ed Robbin followed with a longer piece on Woody's early life in California, concluding: "Fire, tragedy, fatal disease—but don't weep for Woody. He had a rich full life and left a wonderful heritage."[25]

Also in 1976, Dutton finally issued Woody's *Seeds Of Man*. Editor William Doerflinger's wife Joy had worked with Woody on the original publication of *Bound For Glory*. Woody had written various versions of *Seeds Of Man* through the 1940s and into the 1950s, which was "based on an actual trip which Woody took at the age of nineteen with three other members of the Guthrie family: his father, Charlie, his Uncle Jeff, and his older brother,

Roy. But many of the events and characters are imagined or embroidered," Doerflinger explained in his Editorial Note. Focused mostly on his family in Texas and their search for a lost silver and gold mine, *Seeds Of Man* has not generated the popularity of *Bound For Glory*.[26]

As early as 1963 there were plans for a film based on *Bound For Glory*, but Leventhal did not get the financial backing and studio commitment until 1975. *Bound For Glory* was released by United Artists in late 1976 and featured David Caradine as Woody, along with the singing actor Ronny Cox playing a fictional character named Ozark Bule. It focused on Woody's rambling life in California, leaving out his growing radical politics, and the tall Caradine contrasted with Woody's short stature. But Caradine's thin body and rustic appearance embodied how people imagined Woody would have looked. Significantly, Caradine did his own singing while playing Woody. The film received six Academy Award nominations in 1977, and won the Oscars for Haskell Wexler's cinematography and for its musical score. United Artists issued a companion album from the soundtrack.

Warner Bros. Records had produced one of the tribute albums in 1972, and followed up in 1976 with *Woody Guthrie*, all original recordings from the early 1940s, such as "This Land Is Your Land," "Pastures of Plenty," and "Jesus Christ." "He always had an eye for the truth in a situation and when he wrote that truth on in a song he came up with some of the best topical songs, protest songs, children's songs, talking blues and ballads that have ever been written—period," explained Marsha Meyer in Warner Bros.'s promotional magazine. Harold Leventhal, Woody's energized promoter, had the idea for the album once the United Artists film was in production. "Folkways ([Moe] Asch's company) had the largest body of Woody's work," Leventhal explained; "about 40 sides. I figured there would be interest in Woody with the release of the movie, so I went to Moe, who is a good friend, and asked permission to get the widest distribution possible (on these songs). He agreed to permit me to go to Warner Bros. for the distribution deal." This was the real thing: "We've made no changes on (the album), no phony syncs, no new speakers.... We've left in all the scratches, noise and all."[27]

During 1976, the celebration of the Bicentennial of the American Revolution, Asch decided to issue the album *Struggle*. It included the six songs on his original 1946 album, with six additional selections, such as "A Dollar Down and a Dollar A Week" and "Waiting at the Gate." "This album is made possible because Marjorie Guthrie has been after me all these years," Asch explained in the liner notes. "I waited for the Bicentennial to give the struggling people a chance to know that one of their own did not let them down and his songs go on and on and on." At the same time, Jess Pearson, accompanied by group labeled Woody's Friends—Arlo Guthrie, Seals and Crofts, Peter Yarrow (of Peter, Paul and Mary), John Hartford, Ramblin' Jack Elliott, and Hoyt Axton—issued the obscure Cream album (CR-1002) *Woody Guthrie's "We Ain't Down Yet."* Moreover, in October WTTW, the public TV station in Chicago, aired a wonderful *Soundstage* production of *Woody Guthrie's America.* Pete Seeger, Judy Collins, Fred Hellerman (a member of the original Weavers), and Arlo performed Woody's songs, along with the masterful Studs Terkel reading Woody's prose.[28]

By the late 1970s the public perception of Woody's life and achievements had essentially been reduced to that of a rambling bard who had captured the plight of the Okies during the Depression, a footloose character who challenged the social and economic system, then was laid low by a crippling disease for the last fifteen years of his truncated life. One weighty exception was Frederick Turner's lengthy, thoughtful 1977 essay in the popular, hard bound, *American Heritage Magazine.* "Few know and fewer care now that Guthrie wrote some communistic journalism," he cautioned his readers, "that he came to accept the notion that America was in the clutches of a Wall Street-inspired conspiracy against working people, or that he looked forward to the total reorganization of American society as it was then (and now) and to the birth of a new socialistic one out of it." Indeed, Turner stressed "the quintessentially American Woody Guthrie who was almost mystically endowed with a profound understanding of the spirit of this land and whose life and work expressed a fierce and steady devotion to America's promise as a nation founded on the belief in the dignity and divinity of each of us."[29]

The fascinating details of his life were hardly known until Joe Klein published *Woody Guthrie: A Life* in 1980, which would serve as the touchstone for all future studies during the next three decades and fill in many of the gaps in the story. A journalist who had worked for *Rolling Stone* in the late 1970s, Klein had written about Arlo Guthrie for the magazine in 1977. Leventhal liked his work and asked him to write a full-scale biography; Marjorie cooperated by allowing Klein access to her extraordinary cache of Woody's writings. "Woody Guthrie was a man who was born on the frontier and died in the city," Klein noted. "At times, I've been tempted to view his progress from Okemah, Oklahoma, to the Creedmore State Hospital in Queens, New York, as a perverse metaphor for America's progress though the twentieth century—but it really isn't. It is only one life, sad and triumphant and utterly unique, and I have tried to present it as accurately as possible." Using a broad range of documents and interviews, and very well written, Klein at last brought Woody to life as a three-dimensional character, highly creative but also with numerous flaws. He also hints at Woody's importance representing major changes in society through the twentieth century, particularly the move from farm to city, urban growth, ethnic and racial complexities, as well as the various social and economic problems.[30]

To promote his biography, Klein published the article "Woody's Children: He fathered a generation bound for glory and a family bound for tragedy," in *Esquire,* the adult magazine, focusing on his intricate influence. "In a way, Woody's style and attitude had more of an impact than his songs, though each of the new singers knew dozens of Guthrie's lyrics," he deftly explained. "But they seemed particularly interested in recreating the myth of the dusty little stranger who ambles into town, writes a ballad of social significance, gets drunk, seduces a waitress, spends the night in jail, then takes the first freight out the next morning."[31]

In Murray Kempton's insightful review of Woody's life in *The New York Review of Books,* based on Klein's biography, he commented on the disappearance of the radical verses of "This Land Is Your Land," resulting in "the transformation of the song of protest into a hymn of acceptance." Kempton somewhat focused on the years of Woody's wasting away in the hospital, although judging from his family's tragedies, "Doom was thus woven into his destiny. Somewhere, in the wreck of his family when he was a child, he must have sensed the implacability of the appointment of the Guthries with misfortune, and that could explain why his life seems so continual a flight from places whose security could only seem false to him." And Kempton concluded: "The genius of our politics further extends to misunderstanding great lives; and so it was only in accordance with this appointed custom that the young who were anxious to escape their homes made a hero of this man desperate to find one of his own."[32]

Throughout the seventies and into the eighties Woody's recordings became increasingly available and his fame widespread, at least in some circles. In 1984 Harold Leventhal released the documentary film *Woody Guthrie: Hard Travelin',* directed by Jim Brown. "The documentary stops just short of hagiography," *New York Times* music critic Jon Pareles commented in his positive review, "showing all three of Mr. Guthrie's wives (but not mentioning any divorces) and revealing that he drank heavily and was not always fond of bathing. Mostly, however it is a reminder of just how good a songwriter he was. His protest songs and singalong anthems, like 'This Land Is Your Land,' still sound natural, forthright and well-nigh universal." The film's soundtrack included a range of performers doing Woody's songs, including Arlo Guthrie, Jack Elliott, Pete Seeger, Holly Near, Rose Maddox, Hoyt Axton, Ronnie Gilbert, Sonny Terry, and Judy Collins, and appeared on the Arloco label.[33]

Woody's writings were also becoming more accessible, particularly with the 1990 publication of *Pastures Of Plenty: A Self-Portrait, Woody Guthrie,*

edited by Leventhal and Dave Marsh, the rock critic and Bruce Springsteen biographer. Filled with previously unpublished essays and letters, and
chock full of illustrations, it "doesn't just give us Woody the invincible
natural creative force, the politically correct songwriting machine, the
incorrigible optimist, or even, for that matter, the perennially irresponsible hobo and perpetual big city hayseed," Marsh explains. "Every quality in that list assumes vivid existence in these pages but so does another,
equally complex Woody Guthrie: a man who had to struggle for personal
and political responsibility and felt troubled and sometimes even defeated
when he couldn't get a handle on it." Here we are presented with different sides of Woody, which "have been kept concealed by hagiographers
or overlooked by debunkers. Yet these sides of his life and thinking don't
diminish his artistry or his majestic personal integrity." He credits Marjorie Guthrie for taking care of the increasingly ill Woody and his huge
collection of manuscripts and recordings: "If it is true that without Woody
Guthrie there would have been no Bob Dylan, and without Bob Dylan
no popular music, as we understand it today, we owe her an incalculable
debt."[34]

Moe Asch died in 1986, and the following year the Smithsonian Insti-
tution Center for Folklife and Cultural Heritage purchased the complete
Folkways catalog and the owner's papers. To raise the necessary funds for
the collection, soon to be named Smithsonian Folkways, a group of high
powered performers got together to record songs by Woody as well as Lead
Belly. The recordings, and a companion film, came about when Ralph
Rinzler, the folklorist and musician who headed the project, ran into Bob
Dylan, who agreed to get the others involved. Named *Folkways: A Vision
Shared—A Tribute to Woody Guthrie and Leadbelly,* the album included
an amazing array of talent for the Woody selections: Dylan singing "Pretty
Boy Floyd," John Mellencamp on "Do Re Me," Bruce Springsteen perform-
ing "I Ain't Got No Home," U2 doing "Jesus Christ," Arlo singing "East
Texas Red," Willie Nelson doing "Philadelphia Lawyer," Emmylou Har-
ris singing "Hobo's Lullaby," Springsteen again on "Vigilante Man," con-
cluding with Pete Seeger, Doc Watson, and others performing "This Land
Is Your Land." Columbia Records issued the stellar album. Smithsonian
Folkways produced its own companion album, *Original Vision,* with the
original recordings by Woody and Lead Belly. In 1988, the singer-songwriter Larry Long issued an album of songs by and also about Woody, *It
Takes a Lot of People,* on the Flying Fish label.

To encourage the study of Guthrie and Lead Belly, the Smithsonian
Institution Office of Folklore Programs, in conjunction with the Music
Educators National Conference, issued a student workbook in 1991, *A Trib-
ute to Woody Guthrie & Leadbelly,* along with a detailed companion Teach-

ers' Guide. The first included an overview of folk music, short biographies of Guthrie and Lead Belly, introductions to the artists on *A Vision Shared,* plus the words and music to a handful of their songs. "Use these materials to teach about the passion with which Woody and Leadbelly wrote," Rinzler urged the teachers. "It is an infectious passion, full of love for the variety, the creativity, and the rights of humankind." Rinzler mentioned that he "had the privilege of knowing and learning from Woody Guthrie in New York's Washington Square Park—it was Woody who inspired me to take up the mandolin."[35]

Woody's hometown of Okemah had a difficult time in officially recognizing its most famous product, still quite controversial because of his radical politics. After much debate over the years, in 1972 the town agreed to label one of its three water towers "Okemah: Home of Woody Guthrie." The state of Oklahoma admitted Woody to its Music Hall of Fame in 1997, and the next year Okemah initiated an annual Woody Guthrie festival, which is going strong into the twenty-first century. The honors would continue to flow, as the real life Woody receded into the background. In 1998 the U.S. Postal Service honored Woody with a commemorative stamp, part of a strip that included Lead Belly, Josh White, and Sonny Terry. In 2006 the Oklahoma Hall of Fame added Guthrie to its list of great sooners.

Harold Leventhal and the Guthrie family initiated the Woody Guthrie Foundation in 1972, and the Guthrie Archives officially opened in 1996. Woody's daughter Nora, who had been a dancer with little interest in her father's music up to this time, became the Executive Director of the Foundation and Archives. There was an official celebration in Cleveland in late September 1996, "Hard Travelin': The Life and Legacy of Woody Guthrie," with a symposium and two concerts sponsored by the Rock and Roll Hall of Fame and Museum, which had inducted Woody in 1988, along with Lead Belly, Dylan, the Beach Boys, and the Beatles. The more casual concert, held at a nightclub in downtown Cleveland, included the singers Alejandro Escovedo, Jimmie Dale Gilmore, John Wesley Harding, Jorma Kaukonen, Jimmy La Fave Country Joe McDonald, Paul Metsa, and Syd Straw. The more formal affair at Severance Hall the following night featured an amazing lineup, with the British rock singer Billy Bragg, the feminist, folk-punk singer-songwriter Ani DiFranco, Ramblin' Jack Elliott, Arlo Guthrie, the Indigo Girls (Emily Saliers and Amy Ray), David Pirner of the rock band Soul Asylum, Pete Seeger, Bruce Springsteen, with the actor Tim Robbins as master of ceremonies.

"Part tribute to Guthrie through his own music and part tribute through his influence on the perfomers' own songs, the two-and-a-half-hour concert was a celebration of folk music (mostly of the political and social protest variety) of the past 60 or so years," Michael Gallucci explained in

Goldmine. "From Guthrie's contemporaries (Elliott, Seeger), offspring (son Arlo), and disciples (Bruce Springsteen) to the bordering factions of sex (DiFranco, Indigo Girls) and nationality (Brit. Billy Bragg was the only non-American on the bill), it was indeed a tribute to the lasting legacy of Guthrie and his music." This was one of the first indications that Woody's songs could appeal to a younger cohort of pop and rock stars, but the floodgates would soon open. "Most effective was Bragg—modern music's best and most ardent political singer-songwriter—whose UK take on American-derived tunes (two of his songs were previously unpublished Guthrie lyrics that he set to music, 'Unwelcome Guest' and 'Against the Law') was the night's strongest case for the universality of Guthrie's music," Gullucci continued. As for the night's star, "sandwiched between Elliott and Arlo, Springsteen's tender acoustic set included versions of Guthrie's 'Tom Joad' (the two-part song that was the direct inspiration of Springsteen's *Ghost of Tom Joad* album), 'Blowin' Down the Road (I Ain't Going to Be Treated This Way)' with Joe Ely, 'Riding in My Car (Car Song)' (one of the few times during the entire celebration that Guthrie's extensive repertoire of children's tunes was acknowledged) and 'Deportees,' as well as his own 'Across the Border.'"[36]

For those not lucky enough to be in the audience, Ani DiFranco issued a highlights album on her Righteous Babe Records label in 2000. A prolific performer and recording artist, DeFranco selected Ramblin' Jack Elliott performing "1913 Massacre," herself doing "Do Re Me," Arlo singing "Dust Storm Disaster," and Springsteen performing "Deportees." Springsteen had already established himself as another Guthrie (musical and political) disciple, and had performed "This Land Is Your Land" at a concert in Los Angeles in September 1985, when he remarked: "I don't know if you talked to some of the unemployed steel workers ... There are a lot of people out there whose jobs are disappearing. I don't know if they're feeling that this song is true anymore. And I ... I'm not sure if it is, but I know ... I know that it ought to be."[37]

The presentations at the Cleveland symposium were collected by Robert Santelli and Emily Davidson, who had arranged the event for the Rock and Roll Hall of Fame, and published in *Hard Travelin': The Life and Legacy of Woody Guthrie* in 1999. Few academics had tried to research and explore the complexities and ramifications of Woody's life and work, apart from Richard Reuss, but this was now about to change. Indeed, particularly with the opening of the Guthrie Archives, there was a virtual landslide of studies based on a wide range of fascinating materials. In his Preface, Santelli speculated that Woody might have questioned the celebration in Cleveland, since "the ego of America's greatest folksinger was never so large as any one of his songs. And from what I've read about him, he rarely, if ever, put personal glory over, say, the need to rally workers in song or rail against an unjust Establishment."[38]

Whatever Woody might have thought of such attention, the celebrations and studies would continue to pile up. *Hard Travelin'* included interviews with Harold Leventhal and Pete Seeger about their memories of Woody, essays by various academics, and a lengthy bibliography and discography. Dave Marsh added his insightful analysis of Guthrie and race issues: "It's notable that Woody, who more than anyone became the voice of the Okies (to those who believed such people were entitled to or capable of possessing a voice), went out of his way to express racial solidarity whenever he could." Oddly, however, race is hardly mentioned in his published songs (although he had written many anti-racist lyrics), and while he was close to Lead Belly and Sonny Terry, he had a small black following. During his creative life, there were more pressing issues. "To my way of thinking, then," Marsh continues, "one of the most important reasons that there aren't many important Woody Guthrie songs that attack racism and the whole Jim Crow enterprise is that Huntingtons chorea cheated us out of them. The movement to end de jure segregation in the United States began picking up steam in the late forties, but it did so alongside the continuing labor struggles and, equally important, the vicious rampage of the red-baiters and the rise of their anti-Communist blacklist." But if Woody had lived, Marsh has no doubt "that he would have turned his energies to writing for and about the [civil rights] movement.… We cannot know whether he would have matched such Dylan songs as 'The Lonesome Death of Hattie Carroll' and 'Only a Pawn in their Game' in their insights into the system of white supremacy and class manipulation.… We can only know that neither Seeger, nor Dylan, nor any of the other topical songwriters would have done their work in anything like the same way if there had never been Woody Guthrie."[39]

Woody's influences continued to ripple through the musical and political landscape. The activist singer-songwriter Steve Earle, in his 1997 album *El Corazón,* included the haunting "Christmas In Washington," his search for political mentors in this time of trouble. Along with referring to the IWW (Indistrial Workers of the World) bard Joe Hill, the anarchist Emma Goldman, the African American leader Malcolm X, and Martin Luther King, Earle included the plea, "So come back Woody Guthrie to us now."[40]

The opening of the Guthrie Archives in New York City proved a boon for researchers and musicians. "More than 10,000 of his papers, letters, song lyrics, scrapbooks and artworks are being made public for the first time," Peter Applebome announced in the *New York Times* in early 1998. "In the process, his words are finding voice in new forms like a remarkable CD of never-before-heard Guthrie songs filtered through contemporary musical sensibilities." The collection included 700 photographs, 98 scrapbooks, 300 letters, 700 artworks, 700 manuscripts of unpublished songs and poems, and 500 films, videos, and recordings. Considering that Woody traveled so much, this huge collection had survived because of Marjorie's zealous drive to preserve Woody's life. Moreover, since he dated and signed most of his writings, he was certainly conscious about documenting his legacy. "'Woody was not just some guy who played guitar and wrote songs,' Mr. [Jorge] Arevalo [the collection's archivist] said. 'He was the consummate diarist. He was an illustrator, artist, painter. And more than anyone I can think of, he embodies so much of the American spirit, someone who could hang out with blues musicians in the Deep South, migrant workers in California, come to New York and hang out on the Bowery and move in intellectual circles at the same time.'"[41]

The "remarkable CD of never-before-heard Guthrie songs" mentioned in the article referred to "an album due out in June by the English singer-songwriter Billy Bragg, who shares Guthrie's populist, liberal politics, and the American rock bank Wilco, of songs that Guthrie left behind with lyrics but no music.... Mr. Bragg said he had thought the idea a bad one until Ms. [Nora] Guthrie took him into the archive, and he felt immediately sucked in by the richness and depth of the materials."[42]

Born in London in 1957, Bragg formed the punk rock band Riff Raff in 1977, and his first recording appeared in 1983. He went on to produce numerous albums, while becoming deeply involved in British radical politics. "In her original letter to me, Nora talked of breaking the mould, of working with her father to give his words a new sound and a new context," Bragg wrote in the liner notes to *Mermaid Avenue,* his album with Wilco, released by Elektra in 1998. "The result is not a tribute album but a collaboration between Woody Guthrie and a new generation of songwriters who until now had only glimpsed him fleetingly, over the shoulder of Bob Dylan or somewhere in the distance of a Bruce Springsteen song." Moreover, Bragg explained, these songs "offer a broader picture of a man who over the past sixty years has been vilified by the American right while simultaneously being canonized by the American left." Here was not the Okie bard or the Old Left radical, but someone quite different. The songs, such as "Walt Whitman's Niece," "Way Over Yonder in the Minor Key" (which would appear on the soundtrack of the 2010 feature film *Love and Other Drugs*), "Ingrid Bergman," and "Christ For President," demonstrated the range of Woody's intellectual interests. Since there was no music, perhaps they were only written as poems, but whatever Woody's intentions, they were now presented to a fresh audience with little previous introduction to Woody's songs. "I came across a song about a flying saucer," Bragg told Peter Applebome, "which is not what you expect from

Woody Guthrie, and there was a note in the top left-hand corner, with two very un-Woody Guthrie words: 'Supersonic boogie.' Those words opened up the whole project. When you realize Woody Guthrie was writing about flying saucers in 1950, and he wanted the song to be a supersonic boogie, you realize the Woody Guthrie we think we know is not the real Woody Guthrie." Bragg concluded: "They're his songs. Wilco and I just put a nice frame around them, so you can look at them."[43]

Robert Christgau's review in the *New York Times* compared *Mermaid Avenue* with the previously issued *Folkways: A Vision Shared*: "But at a time when roots aficionados bypassed self-defined folk singers for subcultural pop like rockabilly and urban blues, these reinterpretations packed a wallop—they had texture, beat, soul. In the wake of 'Mermaid Avenue,' however, they sound mannered and pious." He praised both Jeff Tweedy, Wilco's lead, and Bragg for an inspiring compilation. The alternative band Wilco had come together in 1994 and had recorded a number of albums before they were approached by Bragg for this project. Bragg's tunes "are even more memorable than those from Mr. Tweedy and Jay Bennett, Wilco's keyboard player," Christgau continued. They have rewritten "history a little, shaking off the inhibitions of the past with a post-modern shrug as it reminds us what hopeful music used to feel like." Nick Krewen, in a review in the *Toronto Star,* praised the album as "a thrilling, eye-opening masterpiece of folk, country and surprisingly apolitical Guthrie tunes." It became a best seller and garnered a Grammy nomination for Best Contemporary Folk Album.[44]

Mermaid Avenue's success prompted Bragg, Wilco, and Nora Guthrie to revisit the collection to produce a sequel, *Mermaid Avenue Vol. II,* in 2000. "Woody Guthrie was the first alternative musician," Bragg expressed in his liner notes. "While Hollywood and Tin Pan Alley were busy peddling escapism to the masses, Woody was out there writing songs from a different point of view with a lyrical poetry that captured the awesome majesty of America's scenery and the dry as dust humor of its working folks." The album included "Airline To Heaven," "My Flying Saucer," "Stetson Kennedy" (about his old friend), and "Joe Dimaggio Done It Again." "These lyrics are but a fragment of a great creative outpouring that occurred in the years after World War II.... When he died, the music he had written for these songs died with him," Bragg explained. [45]

While Bragg and Wilco were putting their distinctive musical stamp on a few dozen of Woody's songs, Nora Guthrie brought another group into the archives to search for Woody's Jewish lyrics. The Klezmatics, having formed in New York in 1986, had been reviving the sound of an Eastern European Jewish musical style, and their first album appeared in 1989. They initially performed Woody's songs in 2003 at a concert in

New York City, "Holy Ground: The Jewish Songs of Woody Guthrie," where they were joined by Arlo, who was raised mostly by his mother and who had a bar mitzvah when he was thirteen, the Jewish coming-of-age ceremony (although as an adult he has had various religious beliefs). "They chose lyrics that spanned Woody Guthrie's moods and interests," Jon Pareles explained in the *New York Times*. "Not all of the songs were about Jewish topics. 'Heaven' was a vision of a worker's paradise with clean factories and no profiteers." But the concert took place on the first night of Hanukkah in December, "and there were plenty of songs for the occasion." Three years later the group released two CDs of some of the songs, *Woody Guthrie's Happy Joyous Hanuka* and *Wonder Wheel*. The first included "Hanuka's Flame," "Hanuka Gelt [money]," "Hanuka Tree," and the title song.[46]

The Klezmatics' *Wonder Wheel* was less culturally Jewish, featuring "Mermaid's Avenue," "Pass Away," "Holy Ground," and "Wheel of Life," songs written from the 1930s into the 1950s; it won a Grammy for the Best Contemporary World Music Album. "Woody Guthrie is primarily identified with the dustbowl Depression of the 1930s," according to the liner notes, but this album "introduces us to a previously little known, intimate aspect of Woody's life; the haven he found in the heymish extended Greenblatt family…. It was comforting for Woody to join their close family life," something he had missed as a child. "Resonating with his essence, the Klezmatics have musically transported these long-lost lyrics to the sacred place they sing about on 'Holy Ground,' a song whose healing powers are all the more remarkable as Woody composed it while in the hospital."[47]

Woody had been deeply influenced by his mother-in-law, Aliza Greenblatt, in the 1940s and began to write songs about Jewish culture. "One time, for instance, I told him, Look, we have a problem," Moe Asch would recall. "There are a lot of things written about Christmas, a lot of things written about the holidays, but there is nothing written about the Jewish holidays that is popular. Why don't you do a Chanukah song, one complete with its social meaning?" Woody quickly wrote "The Ballad of Chanukah." From "*The Bible*, he got the complete story of Chanukah—with the candles and the Maccabees and everything else—and he sang it in terms of an American legend…. Woody Guthrie's personality helped us all to understand that the modern idiom has a lot to do with expressions, that the folk song of today is an expression and a feeling of what we are today." The song did not catch on, but indicated Woody's universal reach. As for his own religious commitment—he had briefly attended the First Methodist Sunday school as a child, but since had little religious affiliation—once when asked his religion, he responded "all or none," but he was steeped in religious history from around the world.[48]

The twenty-first century would witness a flourish of interest in Woody's life and writings, beginning with a traveling exhibition, "This is Your Land: The Life and Legacy of Woody Guthrie." Organized by the Smithsonian Institution Traveling Exhibition Service (SITES) and the Woody Guthrie Archives, it moved around the country. During its stay at The Museum of the City of New York in early 2000, for example, there were a series of panel discussions, films, and a concert. Three years later, celebrating Woody's ninetieth birthday, there were a series of events in Nashville, Tennessee, capped off by a concert at the Ryman Auditorium (original home of the Grand Ole Opry). Bluegrass player Alison Brown joined Guy Clark, Ramblin' Jack Elliott, Nanci Griffith, Arlo Guthrie, Janis Ian, James Talley, and a host of others on the crowded stage. Woody's first wife Mary, his sister Mary, and his original singing partner Maxine "Lefty Lou" Crissman were introduced to the audience, to a standing ovation. In her program notes, Nora Guthrie recalled that she barely knew her ailing father: "I became a dancer, rather than a musician. I discovered rock and roll, and jazz, and avant garde theatre and always kept at least a mile (or more) away from the exploding folk music scene of the '60s." In 1992 she began volunteering at Harold Leventhal's office, where her father's writings were stored, and soon became immersed in the collection and became reconnected to the father she never really knew: "All of his work, all of his songs, his stories, his art, everything he did grew up and blossomed out from one single stem: his pure love of People."[49]

The increasing output of CDs would heighten the circulation of Woody's songs and recordings. Smithsonian Folkways launched a project to digitally issue scores of his original recordings from their collection. Four volumes of "The Asch Recordings" appeared in the late 1990s, making available the heart of his mostly familiar songs in fresh renditions. Geoffrey Himes's review of the second album, *Muleskinner Blues,* argued: "But the main attraction is Guthrie's voice, altering lyrics as it goes along and beaming with the confidence that it can reach out and touch a million anonymous country fans—just as the Carter Family once reached out and touched a young boy from Okemah, Oklahoma."[50]

In 1949 Woody and Marjorie had appeared for a concert in Newark, New Jersey. Despite his large number of concerts, they were rarely recorded—his recordings for Asch and Lomax, for example, were all in studio settings—but this one luckily survived, recorded by a young Rutgers University student. It is particularly unusual because Marjorie, then pregnant with Nora, did the introductions: "As he tunes his old weatherbeaten Gibson acoustic guitar, she begins talking to the audience about him: how his life embodies the 'folk process'; how his travels enabled him to connect with America and the struggles of its people; what it's like to be married to a 'living legend.'" Beginning with "Black Diamond Mine," Woody included "The Great Dust Storm," "Pastures of Plenty," "Goodbye Centralia," and a few others. Titled *The Live Wire: Woody Guthrie,* the CD was packaged with extensive liner notes and received the 2008 Grammy for Best Historical Album.

Joe Klein's biography of Woody had long been the standard for understanding the details of his life. In 2002 Elizabeth Partridge published a popular study, *This Land Was Made for You and Me: The Life Songs of Woody Guthrie,* filled with photographs. Two years later the journalist and folklorist Ed Cray issued *Ramblin' Man: The Life and Times of Woody Guthrie.* Based on extensive research in the Guthrie Archives, plus interviews with a number of Woody's old friends whom Klein had missed, this would now be the starting point for any further research. Mark Allan Jackson's in-depth study of Woody's songs, *Prophet Singer: The Voice and Vision of Woody Guthrie,* appeared in 2007. His artistic life had been essentially overlooked until the publication of Steven Brower and Nora Guthrie's *Woody Guthrie: Art Works* (2005). "His style of drawing mirrors his style of living: fast, spontaneous, impulsive, self-taught, and straight from the heart," Nora explained in her Preface. "They capture both his personal energy, or vibration, and the pulse of everything he saw around him."[51]

Ed Cray next compiled the notes for a four CD set of recently discovered Woody recordings, issued by Rounder Records in 2009. In April 1944 Woody, joined by Cisco Houston and Sonny Terry, did extensive recording for Herbert Harris and Moe Asch, then partners in Stinson Records, but the masters were not uncovered until 2003, although there had been scratchy reissues over the years by both Folkways and Stinson. Here, at last, were clear copies of many of Woody's prime songs, along with detailed notes. "These recordings are treasures," according to Nora Guthrie. "To sit and listen, is to sit with Woody and his crew. And you become part of that crew, you hear how they listen to each other's voices, how they lean in to connect their rhythms and harmonies. It's achingly human simple and direct, yet full of spirited words and ideas.... It's very strange. The more time goes by, the clearer Woody's voice gets."[52]

Woody's songs, old and new, had begun to flood the market into the twenty-first century, with various performers and musical styles, producing a rich outpouring of recordings that Nora Guthrie encouraged. The Vanaver Caravan, a group with Bill Vanaver, John Herald, John Sebastian, and various other musicians and dancers, appeared in conjunction with the traveling exhibit "This Land is Your Land" in New York in 2000. A companion CD quickly appeared, with mostly the older songs, such as "Hard Travelin'," "Vigilante Man," and "Union Maid," but also the previously unrecorded "Gypsies Fortune," "Just One More Time," and "Peace

Pin Boogie," the latter done in a swing style. That same year saw the release of James Talley's *Woody Guthrie and Songs of My Oklahoma Home*. Born in Oklahoma, Talley's own songs had been recorded by Johnny Cash, Johnny Paycheck, Alan Jackson, and Moby. His albums, starting in the 1970s for Capitol Records, had been well received, but *Woody Guthrie* was the only time he recorded someone else's songs. He included such standards as "Belle Starr," "East Texas Red," "I Ain't Got No Home," and "Grand Coulee Dam."

Woody's children's songs had long been celebrated, mostly through recordings by Woody, Cisco Houston, and Pete Seeger. In 1991 Arlo, Joady, and Nora, along with their children, recorded a number of the songs for the 1992 Warner Bros. album *Woody's 20 Grow Big Songs*; Harpercollins simultaneously published an illustrated book with the same title including the songs and Woody's illustrations. The album garnered a Grammy nomination the following year. In 2001 Rounder Records released *Daddy-O Daddy: Rare Family Songs of Woody Guthrie*. It featured a stellar group of performers, including Taj Mahal, Cissy Houston, Billy Bragg and The Blokes, Ramblin' Jack Elliott, as well as Joe Ely and Jimmie Dale Gilmore. The mix of some familiar songs along with those with fresh lyrics includes "Want to See Me Grow," "Don't You Push Me Down," "New Baby Train," "Little Sack O Sugar," and "Curly Headed Baby." At decade's end Sarah Lee Guthrie, Arlo's daughter, along with her husband Johnny Irion, joined by other family members, produced *Go Waggaloo,* thirteen children's songs, with a few written by Woody—"Go Waggaloo," "Bright Clear Day," "Fox and the Goose."

Along with the recordings, a wealth of illustrated children's books began to appear, mostly based on Woody's songs. *This Land Is Your Land,* with paintings by Kathy Jakobsen, was published in 1998, quickly followed by *Bing Blang* (2000), *My Dolly* (2001), *Howdi Do* (2001), and *New Baby Train* (2004). Biographies of Woody aimed at children have included Karen Mueller Coombs, *Woody Guthrie: America's Folksinger* (2002), Anne E. Niemark, *There Ain't Nobody That Can Sing Like Me* (2002), and Bonnie Christensen, *Woody Guthrie: Poet Of The People* (2009). (Of related interest for young people, Gary Galio, with illustrations by Marc Burckhardt, *When Bob Meet Woody: The Story of the Young Bob Dylan,* appeared in 2011.) There was also a wonderful film, *This Land Is Your Land: Animated Kids' Songs of Woody Guthrie* (1997), with a companion CD. Ten years later Peter Frumkin produced a full length documentary film, *American Masters: Woody Guthrie* (2007), which introduced a large TV audience to his fascinating life and musical creations. Moreover, his songs had long been heard on the soundtracks for numerous feature films, documentaries, and TV shows. For example, Michael Moore included "Jesus Christ" for his documentary *Capitalism: A Love Story* (2009), while the same year both the TV series *House M.D.* and *Cold Case* used "This Land Is Your Land" on their soundtracks. In 2008, the comedian Bill Maher featured "Christ For President" in his documentary *Religulous.*

The London-based, punk rock band Alabama 3 (A3) included "Woody Guthrie" on their 2002 CD, *Power in the Blood;* the song is about suffering around the world, but with no mention of Guthrie. The next year two rather odd record albums appeared on German labels. Z-Joe & The Dustbowlers released "A Woody Zombie Hootenanny," while Hans-Eckardt Wenzel recorded *Ticky Tock* in both English and German versions. The first, a German metal band, included familiar titles, such as "Clean-O," "Hard, Ain't It Hard," and "Grassy Grass Grass," but with definitely an unfamiliar sound, at least for traditional Guthrie fans. Wenzel, a German singer-songwriter, visited the Guthrie Archives and selected a group of previously unknown songs, including "He and She," "Been Out On An Ocean Trip," "Every 100 Years," and "Blow, Big Wind."

Meanwhile, back in the United States, the traditional-sounding Joel Rafael Band issued two albums, *Woodeye: Songs Of Woody Guthrie* (2003) and *Woodyboye: Songs Of Woody Guthrie, Vol. II* (2005). Rafael mixed older and newer lyrics, including "Ranger's Command," "Dance Around My Atom Fire," "Circle of Truth," "Ramblin' Around," and "Dance a Little Longer." The singer-songwriter Rafael was joined on vol. II by Jackson Browne, Arlo Guthrie, Jennifer Warnes, and Van Dyke Parks. Rafael also became part of a high powered group of musicians—Jimmy LaFave, Slaid Cleaves, Eliza Gilkyson, Sarah Lee Guthrie, and Johnny Irion, and in the recording Pete Seeger and Fred Hellerman—in the touring group Ribbon of Highway, Endless Skyway, which issued their same named album in 2008. The rich compilation featured "Oklahoma Hills," "Stepstone," "This Morning I Was Born Again," and "Peace Call," among so many others on the two CDs. "People think of him as this hobo Dust Bowl character, riding the rails," LaFave explained. "They don't realize that by the end, he was more like a Beat poet, like (Jack) Kerouac, hanging out in Greenwich Village and Washington Square, writing all this stream-of-consciousness stuff."[53]

The year 2008 witnessed the appearance of Arlo Guthrie and the Dillards' *32 Cents/Postage Due,* filled with familiar titles, such as "East Texas Red," "The Sinking of the Reuben James," "Do Re Mi," and "Ship in the Sky." At the same time Country Joe McDonald released *Tribute to Woody Guthrie,* based on his touring one-man show, with readings along with performing the familiar songs. Beginning with "This Land is Your Land," McDonald added "Talking Dust Bowl," "Riding In My Car," "Slip Knot," ending with "So Long It's Been Good to Know Ya." In 2010, Ray Campi, the longtime rockabilly star, issued *Ramblin' Ray Recalls The Music of Woody: More Hard Travelin'* on the Real Music label. In a different tone, Jonatha Brooke, backed by a group of jazz and pop musicians, mined the Guthrie Archives for her own selection of fresh lyrics, such as "My Sweet and Bitter Bowl," "My Flowers Grow Green," and "King of My Love," for her 2008 Bad Dog Records release. It seemed that whomever dipped into the thousands of known and unknown lyrics came up with their own take on Woody's musical genius.

"If a song isn't finished until the words and music are put together, then the 2,400 lyrics Mr. Guthrie left behind without any recorded or written music are half-songs waiting to be completed," Geoffrey Himes explained in the *New York Times* in 2007. "Those lyrics are now carefully stored in the archives, and every time someone sets them to music, a new song is born." Himes continued: "But the [Billy Bragg] 'Mermaid Avenue' project was merely the kickoff for a songwriting binge that has found Guthrie collaborating from the grave on Hanukkah songs with the Klezmatics, on punk-rock anthems with the Dropkick Muphys, on German cabaret numbers with Wenzel, on Delta blues with Corey Harris, on Texas campfire songs with Joe Ely and Jimmie Dale Gilmore, and on a classical suite with David Amram." The Dropkick Murphys saw Guthrie "as the original punk-rocker, just from the way he lived," and they included Woody's "Gonna Be a Blackout Tonight" on their *Blackout* album (2003) and "I'm Shipping Up to Boston" on *The Warrior's Code* (2005). The latter was also used on the soundtrack for *The Departed,* the 2006 Jack Nicholson feature film. The article concluded: "Whether it's klezmer musicians or hip-hoppers, Ms. [Nora] Guthrie seems determined to prove that her father's lyrics can work in almost any context. 'I'm trying to bring the most unusual suspects into these projects,' she said. 'I'm not doing it to be cute but because these people write to me or get word to me that they've always loved Woody's songs'."[54]

Klee Benally, the son of a traditional Navajo medicine man and a folk singer and songwriter born to Russian-Polish Jewish, formed a punk band, Blackfire, with his two brothers in 1990. "I think that one of the most nervous times I ever had getting on stage was in Okemah, Oklahoma, during the Woody Guthrie Folk Festival," he told interviewer David Dunaway. "Here we are, going to get up there, plug in everything, distortion and all, plug in all our electric amps and everything and look out in the audience. Not to offend anybody but it's all blue-haired [people] with lawn chairs and straw bale seats…. At the end we had a standing ovation…. I don't know what the audience was responding to—maybe they were giving us a standing ovation because we were done! But people came up to us and said, 'You know, Woody Guthrie was a punk-rocker, and if he was around today,

I think he'd like your music too.'" In 2004 Blackfire had recorded the EP *Woody Guthrie Singles*.[55]

Woody's music, indeed Woody himself, was very hard to characterize, part of his personality as well as his legacy. "One day, Woody comes in and squats himself on the floor," Moe Asch recalled of their meetings in the early 1940s. "He squats himself before the office door and just sits there— very wild hair, clean shaven, and clothing one would associate with a West-ern person.... He started to talk—a person of broad English, and then you wonder if that was a put-on. When he lets himself go, his English becomes more common English, with Western or Oklahoman accents. And that's when I know he's not putting me on or making fun. If you listen to those Library of Congress recordings, you can hear all the put-on he wanted to give Alan Lomax. This is the actor acting out the role of the folk singer from Oklahoma. With me, he wasn't at all that way." He should never be typecast, a creative genius, self-educated, who created his own worlds. His legacy reverberated around the world, with an increasing number of musi-cians adopting his songs in their own fashion, with perhaps little thought to copy his quirky style and persona. Moreover, academic studies have continued to be published, for Woody will always serve as a rich subject for any kind of analysis and interpretation, as well as more popular biogra-phies and children's books.[56]

Nora Guthrie has pursued enhancing Woody's legacy well into the twenty-first century: "As caretaker for her father's legacy, she's worked to keep Woody's work relevant for people outside the traditional folk cul-ture, getting his unpublished lyrics into the hands of artists like Wilco and Billy Bragg, the Klezmatics, and Jonatha Brooke, and hiring 20-some-things to work at the Archives who will become the next generation of Woody Guthrie scholars. She gets plenty of unsolicited help from devotees like Bob Dylan and Bruce Springsteen, Tom Morello of Rage Against the Machine, and a host of punk bands that continue to shine a light on Guth-rie as a seminal storyteller and uncompromising political activist." The Guthrie Archives raises funds through collecting copyright permissions as well as individual contributions. In late 2011, 429 Records released *Note of Hope: A Celebration of Woody Guthrie,* with a lineup of Van Dyke Parks, Tom Morello, Lou Reed, Kurt Elling, Jackson Browne, Nellie McKay, and others adapting a range of newly discovered songs.[57]

On February 21, 2011, Morello led the large audience in "This Land Is Your Land" during a mass demonstration in Madison, Wisconsin, protest-ing the Republican governor's attack on public worker unions. The radi-cal Woody has remained alive and well, and appears in full detail in Will Kaufman, *Woody Guthrie: American Radical* (2011), based on a thorough examination of scores of his unpublished songs. Dorian Lynskey's expansive study *33 Revolutions Per Minute: A History of Protest Songs, From Billie Holiday to Green Day* (2011) features Woody in chapter 2, with the focus on "This Land Is Your Land": "Guthrie was a quintessentially American creation—a wanderer, a pioneer, an idealist, a democrat—and his value as an icon of the American left was incalculable." As for children, they can gain an appreciation from Gary Golio's *When Bob Met Woody: The Story of the Young Bob Dylan* (2011), where Guthrie continues to be linked with the pop icon through text and drawings. There is no doubt that books (as well as articles and recordings), for all ages, will continue to appear, perhaps with scant connection to the original, complex Woody Guthrie. Indeed, Guthrie will remain a vital part of the country's musical and cultural heritage long after the centennial anniversary of his birth in 2012, a year filled with conferences, concerts, recordings, publications, and various other tributes to a most singular man.[58]

Pete Seeger should have the last word on his old friend: "I learned so many different things from Woody that I can hardly count them. His ability to identify with the ordinary man and woman, speak their own language without using the fancy words, and never be afraid.... I have traveled around the country and around the world singing his songs, and although Woody was in a hospital for years before his death in 1967, I have always felt he was very much with me, very much alive. I sing his songs with thousands of people, and Woody is right beside me, strumming along. His life is in the words sung from our lips. I know his songs will go on traveling around the world and will be translated into many languages during the coming centuries and will be sung by many people who never heard his name. What better kind of immortality could a man want?"[59]

PART **II**

DOCUMENTS

LETTER FROM WOODIE GUTHRIE TO A FRIEND IN OKLAHOMA, FEBRUARY 1940

Woody had just moved to New York, and in this message to a "friend" he has maintained his folksy personality. The letter refers to his new song, "The Government Road," with the lyrics attached to the letter, which argues that the government should build roads to make life smoother for everybody; it would also create jobs for the unemployed. He never recorded the song, one of the many he kept turning out, which quickly disappeared. He also refers to his antiwar song "Why Do You Stand There in the Rain?," which did become somewhat popular among Communist Party members at the time, until Germany invaded the Soviet Union in June 1941.

––––––––––––––

"This is the first copy of this song ever wrote. It shows you how to write em up without the music. Songs come to me best when walking down the road, and I've got fifteen or twenty road songs, I mean trying to catch a good easy one that everybody can sing the first time you hear it, and fit everybody in the country. The songs New York has liked best so far that I made up is called 'Why Do You Stand There in the Rain?' That is one about the American Youth Congress a going to Washington to stand in the rain and listen to the president. But this one I think is as good because it brings out the idea of plowing down the roots and rocks to build a big smooth road so everybody can travel easier on it, and it would be a government road.

Us Oakies are out of jobs, out of money, out of drinking whiskey, out of everything except hope—and we're walking down that old 66 carrying our work shoes, because our feet are blistered from walking. And since so many folks get killed every day on our narrow minded highways, why don't they pitch in and make them wider? That would at least give us a job. So to the day that we grab our shovels and tractors and build that road, I would like to dedicate this little song. The Government Road. Thank you for the help you gave in buying this first original copy. It was a big help.

> I'm walkin' down that buffalo trail;
> Gonna build a government road;
> Twenty one years I been in jail;
> Gonna build a government road."

Source

Woody Guthrie letter to a friend in Oklahoma, February 1940, from New York City, published in Dave Marsh and Harold Leventhal, eds., *Pastures of Plenty: A Self-Portrait, Woody Guthrie* (New York: HarperCollins, 1990), 37–38.

Letter from Woody Guthrie to Pete Seeger, Millard Lampell, and Lee Hays, July 8, 1941

While Woody was in Oregon writing songs for the Bonneville Power Administration, he kept in touch with his friends in the Almanac Singers in New York, whom he also addresses as "My Beloved Talcum Powder Singers Or Seed Catalog Singers." He details his ideas about the need for updating folk songs, including references to modern technology, which always fascinated him. He also describes his recent concerts, always connecting with his fellow down-and-out Okies as well as the downtrodden city workers. He closely identified with society's unfortunates, and continually thought about how best to connect with them musically.

"No letter received from you and no real reason for writing except to say that I did not get no album of your records which I understand that you sent to me. However if you didn't send none they ain't no hard feeling, because I dont remember of sending but a scant few of my own to anybody and never did own a album of them for over a few minutes at a time.

Boys, what I think need to be done to old time folk songs is not to give over an inch to jazz or swing as far as the melody goes, but what we've got to do is to bring American Folk Songs up to date. This don't mean to complicate our music a tall, but simply to industrialize and mechanize the words. Why should we waste our time trying to wind the calendar back? Our old standby songs were no doubt super stream lined when they first got out, and possibly that is the reason why they spread like a prairie fire. Within my visit to New York I did not have the pleasure of coming across but a mighty few songs of the wheels, whistles, steam, boilers, shafts, cranks, operators, tuggers, pulleys, engines, and all of the well known gadgets that make up a modern factory. Except for just a few work songs of this kind that I heard through Alan Lomax, I am sorry to say the others were almost equal to zero. Alan knew the good of these work songs ten times better than me, and I know that all of you had the jump on me concerning work songs, but this is to simply remind you that the idea is on me like a wild cat with 3 sets of razors in each foot.

I have visited the Oakie camps a time or two since I been out here and they put me on their programs and the crowds were almost too big for you to believe, 600 here, 500 yonder, 300 next place. And they just dam near tore down a perfectly good govt auditorium when I sung about Pretty Boy or Tom Joad. And I made it my business to go into lots of the tents and shacks this trip that I didnt make on other trips, and hear them all sing, the little sisters, brothers, yodlers, ma and pa in the old yaller light of a coal oil lamp, sittin in a rocker, or on the side of an old screaking bed, eyes about half shut, bottom lip pooched out fill of snoose, and they sang religious, hopeful songs and sentimental worried songs but hours on hour could sing and sing and sing. And I made a little speech in each tent and I said, You folks are the best in the West. Why dont you take time out and write up some songs about who you are, where you come from, where all you been, what you was a lookin for, what happened to you on the way, the work you done and the work you do and the work and the things that you want to do. Your songs so far are not your songs, but songs that somebody else has put in your head, and for that matter, not your own life, not your own work, trouble, desires or romances; why had you ought to sing like you're rich when you aint rich, or satisfied when you aint satisfied, or junk like you hear on these nickel machines and over the radio? Every one of them would lean and look towards me and keep so still and such a solemn look on their faces, there in those little old greasy dirty hovels that it would bring the rising sun to tears. In a few minutes some young and dreaming member of the family would break down and say, I been a thinkin about that ever since I commenced a singing. And then the whole bunch would enter into a deeper religious conversation and decide that was right. On more than one night, on more than one day, I've heard my Oakie friends ask me, Say Mister, you dont happen to be Mister Jesus do you? Come back?

Where the works of the Oakies is mainly in following the crops and praying for a little forty of their own, and adopting a mental attitude that it'd all come from a machine that you put a nickel in, the workers in other parts of the country have their mines, mills, croppin farms, factories, etc., from which their songs of their work must come and the answer to Tobacco Road and The Grapes of Wrath. It would be a sorry world if there wasnt no answer. But it is just so arranged that there is an answer, not only to the grinding voices of us Oakies, but to the questions of city workers as well. And it is our job if we claim the smallest distinction as American Folk Lorists, to see to it that the seeds are sown which will grow up into free speech, free singing, and the free pursuit of happiness that is the first and simplest birthright of a free people. For with their songs chocked and their pamphlets condemned, their freedom will be throttled down to less than a walk, and freedom of going and coming, of meeting and discussing, of course, freedom will just be a rich man's word to print in his big papers and holler over his radio, it wont be real, it will only be a word. As now the case about 90% of the time.

I read your war songs and like them a lot. But you ought to throw in more wheels, triggers, springs, bearings, motors, engines, boilers, and factories—because these are the things that arm the workers and these are the source of the final victory of Public Ownership.

Our job aint so much to go way back into history, that already been done, and we caint spare the time to do it all over again. Our job is the Here & Now. Today. This week. This month. This year. But we've got to try and include a Timeless Element in our songs. Something that will not tomorrow be gone with the wind. But something that tomorrow will be as true as it is today. The secret of a lasting song is not the record current event, but this timeless element which may be contained in their chorus or last line or elsewhere."

Source

Woody Guthrie to Pete Seeger, Millard Lampell, and Lee Hays, July 8, 1941, Portland, OR, published in Dave Marsh and Harold Leventhal, eds., *Pastures of Plenty: A Self-Portrait, Woody Guthrie*, New York: HarperCollins, 1990, 53–55.

INTRODUCTION FROM *HARD HITTING SONGS FOR HARD-HIT PEOPLE*

Woody worked closely with Alan Lomax and Pete Seeger to produce their extensive collection of work and political songs, but it was not published until 1967. In his lengthy Introduction, Woody gives a capsule account of his hard scrabble life in the 1930s, then describes the nature of this collection of songs by and about working people. He describes the difficult lives of the farmers and workers, as well as introduces some of the songwriters, such as Aunt Molly Jackson. He welcomes the day when "there ain't no rich men, and there ain't no poor men," which pretty much sums up his political agenda. This is one of the best descriptions of Woody's musical reach and feelings.

"Here's a book of songs that's going to last a mighty long time, because these are the kind of songs that folks make up when they're a-singing about their hard luck, and hard luck is one thing that you sing louder about than you do about boots and saddles, or moons on the river, or cigarettes a shining in the dark.

There's a heap of people in the country that's a having the hardest time of their life right this minute; and songs are just like having babies. You can take either, but you can't fake it, and if you try to fake it, you don't fool anybody except yourself.

For the last eight years I've been a rambling man, from Oklahoma to California and back three times by freight train, highway, and thumb, and I've been stranded, and disbanded, busted, disgusted with people of all sorts, sizes, shapes and calibers—folks that wandered around over the country looking for work, down and out, and hungry half of the time. I've slept on and with them, with their feet in my face and my feet in theirs—in bed rolls with Canadian Lumberjacks, in greasy rotten shacks and tents with the Okies and Arkies that are grazing today over the state of California and Arizona like a herd of lost buffalo with the hot hoof and empty mouth disease.

Then to New York in the month of February, the thumb route, in the snow that blanketed from Big Springs, Texas, north to New York, and south again into even Florida ... Walking down the big road, no job, no money, no home ... no nothing. Nights I slept in jails, and the cells were piled high with young boys, strong men, and old men; and they talked and they sung, and they told you the story of their life how it used to be, how it got to be, how the home went to pieces, how the young wife died or left, how the mother died in the insane asylum, how Dad tried twice to kill himself, and lay flat on his back for 18 months—and then crops got to where they wouldn't bring nothing, work in the factories would kill a dog, work on the belt line killed your soul, work in the cement and limestone quarries withered your lungs, work in the cotton mills shot your feet and legs all to hell, work in the steel mills burned your system up like a gnat that lit in the melting pot, and—always, always had to fight and argue and cuss and swear, and shoot and slaughter and wade mud and sling blood—to try to get a nickel more out of the rich bosses. But out of all of this mixing bowl of hell and high waters by George, the hard working folks have done something that the bosses, his sons, his wives, his whores, and his daughters have failed to do—the working folks have walked bare handed against clubs, gas bombs, billys, blackjacks, saps, knucks, machine guns, and log chains—and they sang their way through the whole dirty mess. and that's why I say the songs in this book will be sung coast to coast acrost the country a hundred years after all nickel photographs have turned back into dust.

I ain't a writer, I want that understood, I'm just a little one-cylinder guitar picker. But I don't get no kick out of these here songs that are imitation and made up by guys that's paid by the week to write 'em up—that reminds me of a crow a settin on a fence post a singing when some guy is a sawing his leg off at the same time. I like the song the old hen sings just before she flogs hell out of you for pestering her young chicks.

This book is a song book of that kind. It's a song book that come from the lungs of the workin' folks—and every little song was easy and simple, but mighty pretty, and it caught on like a whirlwind—it didn't need sheet music, it didn't need nickel phonographs, and it didn't take nothing but a little fanning from the bosses, the landlords, the deputies, and the cops, and the big shots, and the bankers, and the business men to flare up like an oil field on fire, and the big cloud of black smoke turn into a cyclone—and cut a swath straight to the door or the man that started the whole thing, the greedy rich people.

You'll find the songs the hungry farmers sing as they bend their backs and drag their sacks, and split their fingers to pieces grabbing your shirts and dresses out of the thorns on a cotton boil. You'll find the blues. The blues are my favorite, because the blues are the saddest and lonesomest, and say the right thing in a way that most preachers ought to pattern after. All honky tonk and dance hall blues had parents, and those parents was the blues that come from the workers in the factories, mills, mines, crops, orchards, and oil fields—but by the time a blues reaches a honky tonk music box, it is changed from chains to kisses, and from cold prison cell to a warm bed with a hot mama, and from a sunstroke on a chain gang, to a chock house song, or a brand new baby and a bottle of gin.

You'll find a bunch of songs made up by folks back in the hills of old Kentucky. The hills was full of coal. The men was full of pep and wanted to work. But houses wasn't no good, and wages was next to nothing. Kids died like flies. The mothers couldn't pay the doctor, so the doctor didn't come. It was the midwives, the women like old Aunt Molly Jackson, that rolled up her sleeves, spit out the window, grabbed a wash pan in one hand and a armful of old pads and rags, and old newspapers, and dived under the covers and old rotten blankets—to come up with a brand new human being in one hand and a hungry mother in the other, but she took the place of the doctor in 850 cases, because the coal miners didn't have the money.

You'll find the songs that were scribbled down on the margins of almanacs with a penny pencil, and sung to the rhythms of splinters and rocks that the Winchester rifles kicked up in your face as you sang them. I still wonder who was on the tail end of the rifles. Also in the Kentucky Coal Miner Songs, you'll sing the two wrote by Jim Garland, 'Greenback Dollar' and 'Harry Simms,'—a couple of ringtail tooters you're bound to like.

Sarah Ogan, she's the half sister of Aunt Molly, about half as old [and the sister of Jim Garland], and a mighty good worker and singer—she keeps up the spirit of the men that dig for a hamburger in a big black hole in the ground, and are promised pie in the sky when they die and get to heaven, provided they go deep enough in the hole, and stay down there long enough.

Then the next batch of wrong colored eggs to hatch—out pops the New Deal songs—the songs that the people sung when they heard the mighty good sounding promises of a re-shuffle, a honest deck, and a brand new deal from the big shots. A Straight flush, the Ace for One Big Union, the

King for One Happy Family, the Queen for a happy mother with a full cupboard, the Jack for a hard working young man with money enough in his pockets to show his gal a good time, and the ten spot for the ten commandments that are overlooked too damn much by the big boys.

Next you'll run across some songs called 'Songs of the One Big Union'—which is the same Big Union that Abe Lincoln lived for and fought for and died for. Something has happened to that Big Union since Abe Lincoln was here. It has been raped. The Banking men has got their Big Union, and the Land Lords has got their Big Union, and the Merchants has got their Kiwanis and Lions Club, and the Finance Men has got their Big Union, and the Associated Farmers has got their Big Union but down south and out west, on the cotton farms, and working in the orchards and fruit crops it is a jail house offence for a few common everyday workers to form them a Union, and get together for higher wages and honest pay and fair treatment. It's damn funny how all of the big boys are in Big Unions, but they cuss and raise old billy hell when us poor damn working guys try to get together and make us a Working Man's Union. This Book is full of songs that the working folks made up about the beatings and the sluggings and the cheatings and the killings that they got when they said they was going to form them a Working Man's Union. It is a jail house crime for a poor damn working man to even hold a meeting with other working men. They call you a red or a radical or something, and throw you and your family off of the farm and let you starve to death.... These songs will echo that song of starvation till the world looks level—till the world is level—and there ain't no rich men, and there ain't no poor men, and every man on earth is at work and his family is living as human beings instead of like a nest of rats.

A last section of this book is entailed Mulligan Stew which are songs that you make up when you're a trying to speak something that's on your mind ... telling your troubles to the blue sky, or a walkin' down the road with your 2 little kids by the hand, thinking of your wife that's just died with her third one—and you get to speaking your mind—maybe to yourself the first time, then when you get it a little better fixed in your head, and you squeeze out all of the words you don't need, and you boil it down to just a few that tell the whole story of your hard luck.Then you talk it or sing it to somebody you meet in the hobo jungle or stranded high and dry in the skid row section of a big town, or just freshkicked off a Georgia farm, and a going nowhere, just a walkin' along, and a draggin' your feet along in the deep sand, and—then you hear him sing you his song or tell you his tale, and you think, That's a mighty funny thing. His song is just like mine. And my tale is just like his. And everywhere you ramble, under California

R.R. bridges, or the mosquito swamps of Louisiana, or the dustbowl deserts of the Texas plains—it's a different man, a different woman, a different kid a speaking his mind, but it's the same old tale, and the same old song. Maybe different words. Maybe different tune. But it's hard times, and the same hard times. The same big song. This book is that song.

You'll find a section in this book about Prison & Outlaw songs. I know how it is in the states I've rambled through. In the prisons the boys sing about the long, lonesome days in the cold old cell, and the dark nights in the old steeltank and a lot of the best songs you ever heard come from these boys and women that sweat all day in the pea patch, chain gang, a makin' big ones out of little ones, and new roads out of cow trails—new paved roads for a big black limousine to roll over with a lady in a fur coat, and a screwball poodle dog a sniffing at her mouth. Prisoners ain't shooting the bull when they sing a mournful song. It's the real stuff. And they sing about the 'man that took them by the arm,' and about the 'man with the law in his hand,' and about the 'man a settin' up in the jury box,' and the 'man on th' judges bench,' and the 'guard come a walkin' down that graveyard hall,' and about the 'man with th' jail house key,'—and the 'guard a walkin' by my door'—and about the 'sweethearts that walk past the window,' and the old mother that wept and tore her hair, and the father that pleaded at the bar, and the little girl that sets in the moonlight alone, and waits for the sentence to roll by. These outlaws may be using the wrong system when they rob banks and hijack the rich traveler, and shoot their way out of a gamblin' game, and shoot down a man in a jewelry store, or blow down the pawn shop owner, but I think I know what's on these old boys minds. Something like this: 'Two little children a layin' in the bed, both of them so hungry that they cain't lift up their head ...'

I know how it was with me, there's been a many a time that I set around with my head hanging down, broke, clothes no good, old slouchy shoes, and no place to go to have a good time, and no money to spend on the women, and a sleeping in cattle cars like a whiteface steer, and a starving for days at a time up and down the railroad tracks and then a seeing other people all fixed up with a good high rolling car, and good suits of clothes, and high priced whiskey, and more pretty gals than one. Even had money to blow on damn fool rings and necklaces and bracelets around their necks and arms—and I would just set there by the side of the road and think ... Just one of them diamonds would buy a little farm with a nice little house and a water well and a gourd dipper, and forty acres of good bottom land to raise a crop on, and a good rich garden spot next to the house, and a couple of jersey cows with nice big tits, and some chickens to wake me up of a morning and ... the whole picture of the little house and piece of land would go through my head every time I seen a drunk man with three drunk women a driving a big Lincoln Zephyr down the road—with money to burn, and they didn't even know where the money was coming from … yes, siree, it's a mighty tempting thing, mighty tempting.

Now, I might be a little haywired, but I ain't no big hand to like a song because it's pretty, or because it's fancy, or done up with a big smile and a pink ribbon. I'm a man to like songs that ain't sung too good. Big hand to sing songs that ain't really much account, I mean, you know, talking about good music, and fancy runs, and expert music. I like songs, by george, that's sung by folks that ain't expert musicians, and ain't able to read music, don't know one note from another'n, and—say something that amounts to something. That a way you can say what you got to say just singing it and if you use the same dern tune, or change it around twice, and turn it upside down, why that still don't amount to a dern, you have spoke what you had to speak, and if folks don't like the music, well, you can still pass better than some political speakers.

But it just so happens that these songs here, they're pretty, they're easy, they got something to say, and they say it in a way you can understand, and if you go off somewhere and change 'em around a little but, well, that don't hurt nothin'. Maybe you got a new song. You have, if you said what you really had to say—about how the old world looks to you, or how it ought to be fixed.

Hells bells, I'm a going to fool around here and make a song writer out of you. No, I couldn't do that—wouldn't do it if I could. I ruther have you just like you are. You are a songbird right this minute. Today you're a better songbird than you was yesterday, 'cause you know a little bit more, you seen a little bit more, and all you got to do is just park yourself under a shade tree, or maybe at a desk, if you still got a desk, and haul off and write down some way you think this old world could be fixed so's it would be twice as level and half as steep, and take the knocks out of it, and grind the valves, and tighten the rods, and take up the bearings, and put a boot in the casing, and make the whole trip a little bit smoother, and a little bit more like a trip instead of a trap.

It wouldn't have to be fancy words. It wouldn't have to be a fancy tune. The fancier it is the worse it is. The plainer it is the easier it is, and the easier it is, the better it is—and the words don't even have to be spelt right.

You can write it down with the stub of a burnt match, or with an old chewed up penny pencil, on the back of a sack, or on the edge of a almanac, or you could pitch in and write your walls full of your own songs. They don't even have to rhyme to suit me. If they don't rhyme a tall, well, then it's prose, and all of the college boys will study on it for a couple of hundred years, and because they cain't make heads nor tails of it, they'll swear you're a natural born song writer, maybe call you a natural born genius.

This book is songs like that. If your're too highbrow for that, you can take your pants and go home right now, but please leave the book—some people might want to look through it.

If you're so rich that you look down on these kind of songs, that's a dam good sign you're a standing on your head, and I would suggest that you leave your pocketbook and wife and ice box and dog and catch out east on a west bound freight, and rattle around over this United States for a year or so, and meet and see and get to knowing the people, and if you will drop my a postal card, and enclose a 3¢ Uncle Sam Postage Stamp—strawberry or grape, either one, both flavors are good—why, I'll send you back a full and complete list of the addresses of the railroad bridges that 500,000 of my relatives are stranded under right this minute. (From east coast to west coast, and I ain't a coastin', I mean, I ain't a boasting.) It's the—it's you wax dummies in the glass cases I'm a roasting. If you are one, you know it already, I don't have to sing it to you, and I don't have to preach it to you, your own song is in your own heart, and the reason you're so damn mixed up and sad, and high tempered and high strung, it's because that song is always a ringing in your own ears—and it's your own song, you made it up, you added a verse here, and a verse yonder, and a word now, and a word then—till—you don't need a book tellin' about songs, yours is already ringing and singing in your ears.

The only trouble is with you, you hold it back, you hide it, you keep it down, you kick it down, you sing over it, and under it, and off to all four sides, and you get out on limbs and you sing it, and you get lost in so called arts and sciences and all sorts of high fangled stuff like 'intellect' and 'inspiration' and 'religion' and 'business' and 'reputation' and 'pride' and 'me'—and you say, talk, live, breathe, and exercise everything in the world, except that real old song that's in your heart.

Thank heaven, one day we'll all find out that all of our songs was just little notes in a great big song, and when we do, the rich will disappear like the morning fog, and the poor will vanish like a drunkard's dream—and we'll all be one big happy family, waking up with the chickens, chickens we don't owe nothing on, and a skipping through the morning dew, just as far as you want to skip.

I've got off of the subject 719 times in less than 15 pages, I told you I ain't no good as a writer, but—well, looks like you're already this far along and I feel so sorry for you a having to try to wade through my writing like a barefooted kid through a sand-burr patch—think I'll just thank you for your visit, borrow fifty cents if you got it to spare, and try to throw some sort of trash or weeks or rags or something on this internal typewriter— and maybe it'll sort of quit."

Source

Woody Guthrie, "Introduction," Alan Lomax, Woody Guthrie, Pete Seeger, *Hard Hitting Songs for Hard-Hit People*. New York: Oak Publications, 1967, (originally written in 1941), 15–20.

"Living & Dying & Singing,"
an essay by Woody Guthrie

Woody seemed to write about everyone and everything. In this essay, unpublished during his lifetime, he continues to identify with the poor, black and white, and denounces the rich. He connects people's lives with the current popular songs, which he finds unconcerned with real world problems. He would prefer songs that contain the language of the masses. Woody was always defending songs that made sense, that referred to making a better world, not those that just made money.

"The way I figure, there are two kinds of singing and two kinds of songs. Living songs and dying songs. There's all kinds of living and all kinds of dying. Out in Hollywood they have a place that doesn't do anything but make up lunches for dogs—every day a different meal, every meal balanced and tested for vitamins. The movie stars shell out $20 a week and every day a shiny white truck drives up and delivers the dog's lunch. That's one kind of dying.

Down in east Arkansas the Negro leader of a sharecropper tent colony was beaten to death by vigilantes. He led his people out on strike and the vigilantes beat the side of his head in. They did it with clubs. They slammed him in the groin and his testicles swelled to the size of footballs. The old man lay on a heap of rags and blankets dying, and the whole colony gathered around. He told them, 'They got ouah hands tied. Unite us and see what we can do!' Then he died. That's one way of living.

The dying songs—the ones about champagne for two and moon over Miami—you hear them on the juke boxes, in the movies and over the radio.

That's because the guys who run the juke boxes and the radio want to pass out dying songs. Songs that tell working people, 'There's nothing in work that's any good. Nothing in your life is decent. So keep still and listen to us—we're the artists, the singers, the musicians. Some day, if you're good, and work hard, you'll get to the boss. Then you can wear white tie and tails and have songs made up about you.' That's what the dying songs say.

History Singing

Whatever has happened here or yonder, it's left us plenty to talk and sing about.

Po' Howard's dead and gone,
Left me here to sing this song;
Po' Howard's dead and gone,
Left me here to sing this song!

Listen to your radio. Go to the movies. Play your phonograph records. Go down to the record shop and take a look at the titles, play them over, and listen. What percent of these songs would you call rock-bottom American? What would you say was really worth having around the house? What percent say most, anything at all, or least about politics? What about work, hours, wages, prices, love, marriage, kids, groceries and school? What about making a better world to live in by fixing the one we got?

Which song makes the best? What are the rules for making a song of this calibre? Can you write an American Folk Song? Will your song last? Will people keep singing it after you're down in the cypress grove? Has America got a history worth singing about? Is the history of today, the fast-traveling current events of this very minute, worth singing about? What section of the American people are carrying the real load, doing the real work, the real fighting, the real living, loving, courting, and song-making right this minute? Who is keeping American history alive and moving? Who is holding progress back? Who is going forward and who is drifting backward?

What do you think about the average run of Hollywood and Broadway stuff? Is Tin Pan Alley a full-blooded American? Are all showfolks screwball? Artists, too? Where do they get that way? Who pays some actors and artists such ungodly high wages, and why?

Are songs hard to write, sing, and spread? What do you write them about? Where do you go to sing them? Who'll back you? Where do you find the material? Ideas? People to listen?

Why do some songs spread so fast and last so long? Why do others fall by the side of the track. Do the leading song writers, like radio script writers, take it for granted that we've got a 11-year-old mind? What do kids think about our old-time songs and ballads? Do the 'Hits of the Week' give a decent picture of life in America as she is lived? Is there an actual, outright frameup to control the making up and the spreading around of songs, stories, plays, articles?

Is Organized Labor big enough and smart enough to furnish its own self with entertainment of all kinds; can union dollars be spent entirely in union night clubs, halls, and theaters that deal 100% with the striking, picketing, marching, militant history of Trade Unions in the United States? How far toward Hollywood or B'way can any kind of a talented person go, and still keep in touch with, and honest to, the working people?

Where have theater groups lost the scent of the trail in the past? What has gone out of people's theaters in the past? Why did they scatter, and fold up? Who went where? Where can you find the new sprouts, what are they doing, and what have they learned from past experience? Do Longshoremen, Inland Boatmen, Teamsters, Truck Drivers, Steel Workers, Auto Workers, Warehousemen, Seamen, Ladies Garment Workers, Ladies Auxiliaries, etc., like the average run of people's theater well enough to get worked up about it and get in back of it, and keep it growing …? If not, why not? If so, why?

Who could you call the masses of people? What part do they play in any cultural job to be done? What do people want? Are they looking for 'something' in their entertainment, and not finding it? What is that certain 'something,' and will people 'know' it when they run onto it?

What about the word 'contact' with the people? Is there a 'contact'? Is it a place, a condition, or a state of mind? Is it like a piece of string that is easy to break? Does an education cut you loose from your people? Is it better to stay ignorant and be natural? With a union education, will folks gradually give (working class) artists better backing, and a bigger, freer, market for better work?

Do the broad masses of people have a 'language'? What is it? Is it a proposition of forgetting your accent and just naturally being honest, straight, upright, etc.? Can this 'language' of the masses be wrote down in a dictionary? When you hear workers everywhere staying Buddy, listen, you talk our lingo, see … what do they mean? What part have songs played in making this language, keeping it going, and making it easier to savvy? What sort of lingo sticks in a song and what sort peters out? Where 'bouts along Broadway does this language get louder and louder, but faker and faker? Why is this the natural thing in the show biz as she is run? Who makes money out of it? Who pays the bills? Is it high priced? How could a

Trade Union theater use exactly this same kind of lingo and still keep on a solid footing?"

Source

Woody Guthrie, "Living & Dying & Singing," ca. 1946, published in Harold Leventhal & Marjorie Guthrie, eds., *Woody Guthrie Songbook*. New York: Grosset & Dunlap, 1976, 30–31, 34–35, 39.

"Remembering Woody," by Pete Seeger

Pete Seeger early became Woody's close friend, and remained so until his death in 1967. This essay, published while Woody was still alive, but incapacitated in the hospital, gives a brief overview of Woody's life, as Pete understood it. He gives details, as well, about their early friendship. This is a sensitive memory, full of respect and admiration, although with some admission of Woody's personal faults. There were few others who had such a close relationship with Woody and who could express such feelings.

"I don't think I knew Woody better and longer than other people. There was Cisco Houston, for example, and Jim Longhi who was with him in the Merchant Marine, but I'll do my best to tell you what I can.

Woody has described his own musical education pretty well. The lonesome old ballads sung by his mother, the honkytonk blues, and the wild hollers that he heard from his father and other men in town. And speciallly, I think it worth emphasizing that his style of guitar picking he picked straight off the recordings of the Carter Family, which were so popular around 1931 when Woody was 18 years old. He also learnt some of his favorite songs directly off their recordings. Another favorite of his, of course, Jimmy Rodgers, 'the yodeling brakeman.' And Woody also used to accompany his uncle Jeff, who was a fiddler, and they played on the radio occasionally. And so you see he fits right in with the '20's and '30's. So much so, that I know some people in New York when they first heard him would say to me, 'Why, he's just a hillbilly singer, isn't he?' But like most country musicians Woody was also interested in topical material. And so just as Jimmy Rodgers has songs about his T.B., it was the most natural thing in the world for Woody to make up songs about the Dust Storms.

Thus, after he had gone to California and was singing for $1 a day, I believe, on a Los Angeles radio station, he attracted the attention of a man who was a news commentator for a newspaper, the 'People's World,' over the same radio station. This man got interested in him and his ideas. Woody was introduced to Will Geer, the actor, who was doing some benefits to try and raise money for the migratory labor camps. Woody came along and dived into the struggle. He became a close friend of Will Geer and his family. Through Will, Woody started to make a living singing at fund raising parties around Los Angeles. Will sent to me a copy of Woody's mimeographed songbook 'On A Slow Train Through California,' and told me I sure ought to meet Woody when he came to New York, as he did the following year, 1939.

When I met Woody I was just starting to try and learn how to pick a banjo. I was working for Alan Lomax down in the Library of Congress in Washington, D.C., and Woody came through there several times. Usually on some kind of booking or other. We seemed to hit it off pretty well together, and around April, 1940, as I remember, Woody came down driving a car which he hadn't finished paying for, and asked me if I'd like to come with him to Oklahoma. So I quit my job—such as it was—and we 'hitch-hiked on credit,' as he said, down through Virginia and Tennessee on to Oklahoma, and then to Pampa, Texas, where Woody's wife and children were staying with her parents.

I don't think we stayed in Pampa more than a week or two, and then went back to Oklahoma City, where the finance company came and took his car, as I remember it. We went back east with Bob Wood, and were learning things all the way.

I spent the rest of 1940 hitch-hiking by myself. Woody rejoined his family on the West Coast and went to work writing songs for the Bonneville Power Administration. In 1941, Lee Hays, Mill Lampell, and myself started the Almanac Singers. Woody joined us in June of that year. The Almanacs toured west and came back. In the fall of 1941 we started a co-operative apartment, Almanac House, where people came and went all the time. The cuisine was erratic but interesting; the furniture and decorations practically non-existent; the sleeping done at very odd hours. But the output of songs was phenomenal. We got bookings for $5 here and occasionally $10 there, and by working hard just managed to keep body and soul together. On Sunday afternoons we held open house. 35¢ was charged at the door, and we and friends would sing all afternoon. We called 'em 'Hootenannies'—a term Woody and I had picked up in Seattle.

Once in a long while we'd get a radio job. It was as the result of one of these radio jobs that an agent working for the William Morris Agency got interested in us.

He took us up to the Rainbow Room, which was at that time a top New York night club at Rockefeller Center. We sang a few songs over the mike that afternoon while the bored manager sat in the empty nightclub. He said he might be interested in having us work there, but we had to 'make the act look better.' The men should all wear one-suspender overalls and the women members of the Almanac wear sunbonnets and gunnysack dresses. We didn't take too kindly to that suggestion and started improvising some verses which Woody mentioned in *Bound For Glory*:

> At the Rainbow Room the songs on to boil,
> They're stirring the salad with Standard Oil.
> And: The Rainbow Room it's mighty high,
> You can see John D. a-flying' by.
> Oh, and this one:
> The Rainbow Room's sixty stories high, they say,
> It's a long way back to the U.S.A.

Well, we walked out of there not really expecting that they'd want to hire us, and not really wanting to work there on his terms. Furthermore, right after that we were red-baited in one of the New York papers—the *World-Telegram*, I think—and the agent quit trying to get us any work.

While I can't speak for Woody, I would say that while he didn't chase after commercial work, he'd be perfectly willing to accept a commercial job, not only because it brought him some money but it helped him reach people. He would quit the job if it started to interfere with anything else he wanted to do. In 1939 [1940] he had a job paying $200 a week—which was a lot of money then—to sing one song or two per week for the Model Tobacco network radio program. If he'd been willing to play along with them and sing the songs they wanted him to sing (and not sing the songs they didn't want him to sing), and quit doing leftwing bookings on the side, he could have stayed with them and had a successful commercial career. But he quit after about a month or two at most, I believe.

I guess Woody can express his feelings on this point, and although this was not written specifically in reference to his leaving the Model Tobacco show, I think it shows his feelings of what came first. It was written in 1941:

> The worst thing that can happen to you is to cut yourself loose from people. And the best thing is to sort of vaccinate yourself right into the big streams and blood of the people.

To feel like you know the best and the worst of folks that you see everywhere and never to feel weak or lost, or even lonesome anywhere.

There is just one thing that can cut you to drifting from the people, and that's any brand or style of greed.

There is just one way to save yourself, and that's to get together and work and fight for everybody.

Incidentally, there's an interesting little story about how Woody got around to writing the book 'Bound for Glory.' It all starts with the fact that I once had a job as a cook in 1938 when I was a Harvard student. The man I was cooking for was a bachelor living on Beacon Hill. And one night we had some Harvard instructors in for dinner. He was active in the Teacher's Union in Harvard, and his name was Charles Olson. I understand he is now a fairly well known critic and poet. Big tall man. Anyway, in Greenwich Village in 1942, four years later I meet him and invite him up to supper at Almanac House. He meets Woody and is fascinated, and asks Woody to write an article for a little magazine he was helping on called *Common Ground*. The article was called 'Ear Music' and was a beautiful piece of Woody's genius. 'A definition of folk music by one of the folks.' The article was so well received that a number of people suggested that Woody write a book. And before we knew it, he started work on 'Bound for Glory.' I can't tell you the rest of the story because by the time the book finally reached print I was in the Army.

What do I think of Woody as a writer? Well, he *was* a genius. All of a piece. He wasn't pretending to be anybody else—he was just himself. Like Popeye, 'I yam what I yam what I yam.' He wrote fairly fast and his big problem was that he had not learned how to rewrite and boil down later on. He learnt from everybody, and from everything. He learnt from the King James Bible; he learnt from the leftwing newspapers and publications; he learnt from reading Rabelais. At the same time he was highly selective and knew when he disapproved of something and was going to steer clear of it. He once wrote, 'I must remember to steer clear of Walt Whitman's swimmy waters.'

About Woody's personal life. Woody had an itching heel, there's no doubt about it. I guess I first learned what an undependable husband Woody must have been when we visited his family in Pampa Texas in late 1940. Mary, Woody's wife, I think gave up on Woody when he called it quits on his job with the Bonneville Power Administration. She went back to Texas.

Is that the price of genius? Is it worth paying? Maybe it's easy for me to ask that. It wouldn't be as easy for poor Mary, who was trying to build a home and a family.

But I don't think it's up to me to pontificate, and decide what a creative person should do and should not do. Except to observe that some creative people have created by staying in one place as did Cezanne, the painter, and Thoreau, who once said, 'I have traveled widely in Concord." There are other creative people who must travel a great deal and continually make it hard in other ways on friends and family. Like Robert Burns, Gauguin, Hemingway and Lord knows how many others.

I learned a helluva a lot from Woody. As a person and as a musician. My guess is that different people were able to learn different things from him. The most valuable thing I learnt from Woody was his strong sense of right and wrong, good and bad his frankness in speaking out, and his strong sense of identification with all the hard-working men and women of the world."

Source

Pete Seeger, "Remembering Woody," *Mainstream,* vol. 16, no. 8, August 1963, 27–31. Based on an interview with Josh Dunson.

"The Debt I Owe,"
an essay by Woody Guthrie

By the late 1940s, when this was written, Woody closely identified with Coney Island and his new, Jewish, family, the Greenblatts. This essay was apparently designed as a larger exploration of his wife Marjorie's family. While Woody's life is usually connected with his Okie background then life in New York's politically activist world, by this time he had become steeped in Yiddish culture and was a dedicated family man, as much as that was possible. He also refers to his war record and the destruction of World War II. By now he had also dropped his folksy writing style, which had always been a fabrication. Here is a Woody hardly hinted at in his popular image.

———————

"Every day, and several times a day, a thought comes over me that I owe more debts than I can ever pay back.

I walked around the streets here of Coney Island and I look in at every window, windows of the stores, windows of houses, in the doorways and steps, and I feel this debt I owe. I walked home tonight from a movie that showed the people on the Waterloo Bridge in London during a couple of air raids, and all through the movie, this feeling ran through me. You see, I've seen that Waterloo Bridge in London, I've seen their Waterloo Railroad Station while the Buzz bombs, those Nazi Rocket bombs, were jarring the rocks, the concrete, the iron works, and tonight I feel my terrible debt plainer than I could see it ever before.

The feeling is a crazy mixed up whirl, a world of fallen wreckage, a garbage heap, a tangled, wild sort of a salvage yard, a vision called up by a loose blown paper, a curb stone of gum wrappers, stuck matches, empty paper cups, the smell of trash cans, the looks on every face, the ways that people hump, stroll, saunter, and crawl along the sidewalks. It comes over me like a mist rising or a fog falling, like a danger bell ringing out here in the channel.

When it hits me I see not only my three Invasions and two torpedoes of my days in the merchant marines, not only my eight months I spent in the Army Air Corps, but I see my whole life stretched out in back of me. I owe everybody this same debt.

I wonder some times when my new found feeling comes how I can ever pay any such debt, I mean, such a debt as you can't even see, only feel, only know, but can't speak about it. And when I feel this way, I feel the same way that Marjorie feels when she cries.

I got a few good hard whippings when I was a kid back in Oklahoma. The first few beatings made me cry, not about the hurt of the strap or the stick, but just to think that the whipper really believed in his whip. The next few flailings I cried lots louder, to bet the whipper to take pity on me and stop. The last few, I didn't cry at all. I've never been able to really break down and cry anymore since then.

I've heard Marjorie cry plenty of times in our 5 years together. I tell her I wish to my soul that I could just break down and cry a few times a day. I've seen our daughter, 3 1/2, Miss Cathy, cry like a baby, like a devil, like an angel, cry just like her mommy cries.

Nobody will ever know how much I would give just to have that first gift and clean talent it takes to turn on your tears and cry. No eyes shine quite as bright as your own while you are having a real good cry. It always looked like to me that you can see how honest a person is by watching them cry. But, if this is true, then I must not be a very honest man.

Oh, I guess I do cry. I guess I cry inside of my own self somewhere. I suppose I cry down here on paper. Ink and tears run just about the same rip tides.

A torpedo knocks a lot of things out of you, and if you live through the shake up, it knocks a lot of new things into you. It puts a lot of your thoughts straighter in your mind, and sets your hopes and your plans up clearer and plainer. If I had sunk down in the waters I know that I would have gone on down saying, 'Take it easy, but take it' and, if I had plenty of water and time to make a longer speech I'd have said, as I've always said, 'This world is your world and my world, take it easy, but take it.'

This is not a tale, though, about cute sayings. This is not a tale about funny wise cracks. I can't make it a story about wise proverbs, nor sound advice. I can't write down an outline of it, not give it a shape nor a plot.

I can't write it down like it was a love diary nor a daily cash book. I can't get it said if I put it inside a frame, because there's not a frame in the world big enough nor costly enough to hold it.

You'll just have to be my expert listener, my psychic doctor or just my good friend, and act like I am paying you Seven Dollars an hour just to listen to me spout off. And if I don't get it said to where it makes sense, and if you don't listen, well I'll get it up and I'll walk down under the Coney Island boardwalk, on down to the ocean's damp sands, and start walking. I'll walk a thousand miles around the breaking waves, and I'll hum my story and my feeling to every empty life jacket that I see float in.

I'll start with Marjorie. I'll take you through her dance studios and stages. I'll take you out and lead you by the finger through our three Invasions, through our two torpedoes, through air raids, V Bomb raids, through the magnetic mines, through the wet poker decks, and on through the oil strangled sailors, and on through our walks across north Africa, the mountains of Sicily, the heather hills of Scotland, the hard oak of Wales, the peat bogs of Ireland, the old rock houses of Liverpool and those grey slate rooftops across London, and then back home again on the hospital ship, and always back between ships to Marjorie and to Cathy. I give you my word I won't harm you nor hurt you. I'll take you through eight months of Army camps and bring you right back to Cathy and Marjorie.

Marjorie is small in size. Her hair is thick, shiny, curly and sparkles when she shampoos the big city soot out of it. Since the day she was born twenty nine years ago she has kept on dancing, except for a few weeks here and there of busted ankles, blistered feet, bones and muscles out of joint, and ligaments and gristles pulled out of socket. Even when her body was too bruised and broken, her face, her eyes, her mind has gone on dancing.

Her mother is Aliza Greenblatt, a fine Yiddish folk singer and well known poetess. I doubt if Mrs. Greenblatt ever took three strong drinks of spirits in her life. She is more of a fine actress than anybody admits, and can take a whole afternoon to act out a whole tragic comedy, playing all of the characters, mama, papa, neighbor, sister, brother, aunt, uncle, grandpa, grandmama, visitor, friend, rabbi and all, while her blackmarket chicken burns to ashes in the new modern oven. Aliza Greenblatt has been moulded by sculptors, painted by artists, sung by poets and toasted by drinkers, recorded by recorders, and published in song books. She has that moving and living fire in her face and in her eyes that same sort of an honest strength about her that you could see in the movement and hear in the words of Franklin Delano Roosevelt. She was born in a little town somewhere in Roumania, was raised there, married there, and came to the U.S. along at this same time.

Isadore Greenblatt met Aliza at the gang blank, took her to their first home in Coney Island where he turned the pages of radical and anarchist books, as well as big thick ones about Capital and Labor, Socialism, Trade Unionism, and Communism, as well as through the several kinds of religious books, pamphlets, newspapers, and text books of the history, growth, evolution, birth and life of the whole race of humans. He walked the streets by day as a street peddler, sold ties, handkerchiefs, and novelties of every useful sort. By night he was mostly at home again with his new found wife and the words printed down on his pages in Hebrew, Jewish, Yiddish, and English. His walking by day with his pack of wares kept his feet strong, his appetite good, and his body full of life, spring, bounce. He craved to learn more and more and then to learn some more. His books were his wine, his drink was hot tea and lemon juice. By hard work and honest sweat, Isadore Greenblatt worked his way from a small street peddler, to a busy dry goods salesman covering several large cities. He kept his good health and worked his way on and on, up and up, till he came to be the owner of a fair sized clothing factory. He tried to be as honest as the day is long, and his less honest friends and relatives cashed in on the fat and licked up all of the gravy. They had good union spirit and free working conditions in Izzy's factory and he liked for his workers to have a good union. It made them work and feel better. But closer friends and finer relatives stole him broke and borrowed him flat. He lost his factory and all of the work hands cried to see him go. He tried to go to make his friends and relatives pay him back, but treated them so nice that they put off their payments. Isadore took up his grips and suit cases full of dry goods samples and went back to the trains and the big towns to get him and his family a fresh start. Money came and money went in some awful funny ways to Isadore and Aliza Greenblatt. Every single night, and at odd hours out of each new day, Isadore turned through the thick books that told all about good folks, bad folks, politics, economics, business, money, religion, and salesmanship."

Source

Woody Guthrie, "The Debt I Owe," October 25, 1946, published in Dave Marsh and Harold Leventhal, eds., *Pastures of Plenty: A Self-Portrait, Woody Guthrie.* New York: HarperCollins, 1990, 86–90.

"Singing, Dancing and Team-Work," an essay by Woody Guthrie

Woody's relationship with Marjorie Greenblatt also connected him with the modern dance scene in New York. In this 1942 unpublished essay, he explores his difficulties in accompanying the dancers, since he was an undisciplined musician. He was fascinated by the dancers and their movements, but quickly realized the problems of blending with them musically, despite the popularity of his songs. Here is yet another side of Woody's interests and personality.

"I've had a funny problem here lately. Working with a group of dancers, the New Dance Group.

My special problem was to sing some old time songs count for count and beat for beat as they were on some records. The New Dance Group had been rehearsing their dances by the use of a phonograph and they'd created and built their dances in this way.

I couldn't possibly have been with the dancers on all of the days because of my work of writing and making up songs and singing at different places kept me busy. My trouble wasn't that I didn't know the songs because I'd known all of them for years.

But it was here that I learned a funny thing. People that sing folk songs never sing them twice alike. If you're the same the weather's different and if the weather is the same and even you're the same, you breathe different, and if you breath the same you rest or pause different. The problem I had was to memorize these folk songs according to exactly as they were on the records.

One of the records was my own. A commercial record called I Ride An Old Paint. Imagine how funny I felt trying to sing this song in exactly the same speed and rhythm as I did on the rainy afternoon that I recorded it in the studios of the General Record Company. I was on my way out of town with the group of singers who got to be so well known 'The Almanac Singers.' We were headed for Frisco and the whole West Coast—we had an old 1931 Buick rattletrap car—and we was all in a rush and a push and we needed some money to buy gas because our old car was mortally a gas eater. We had 3 thousand 500 miles to travel and at the last minute we got the job making the two albums of records for this particular company. We shut ourselves up in the studio and sung the songs over a few times and the man cut them unto records. Then he played them back for us and we all stood and listened to the songs and then we run and jumped in our junk heap and took off and I never heard of the songs or the records again till several months later—after our Almanac tour—I was back in New York and the New Dance Group called at my living quarters because there was a big empty hall with a hardwood floor and we all got limbered up and tried the songs along with the dance they had worked out.

First they played the records on a phonograph and went through the dances. I watched their pretty bodies and wished I was a dancer. I swore to quit whiskey and tobacco and start out taking physical exercise. I next tried to sing the same songs but I sung them all wrong. I sung them according to my old philosophy of 'inspiration' and 'feeling' but I sung the wrong counts, paused wrong, got the speed wrong and the time wrong. I figured a dancer with any sense at all could make a few quick changes and invent a few steps if he had to in order to keep in step with my singing.

The dancers tried to do exactly this and they bumped and tromped on one another and flailed their fists and heads together and poked each other in the ribs and faces and in the small of the back with their elbows.

I learned a good lesson here in team work, cooperation, and also in uniform organization. I saw why socialism is the only hope for any of us, because I was singing under the old rules of 'everyman for his self' and the dancers was working according to a plan and a hope. (I learned that a planned world is what you need.)

I was nervous and scared. The dancers looked so good and so hard working and so honest. The old hall was fogging full of dust from between the cracks and I got my mouth full of dust everytime I laid my head back and my mouth open to sing. My hair was catching dirt and trash out of the air. The dancers all tried it over and over. I watched them puff and sweat and slave and work. Dirt stuck to them and they looked like statues dancing.

I would do all right for a while and then I'd miss a beat or put in a note too many and everybody would run over everybody else.

Because of a shortage of life insurance policies and in order to save human lives for the war effort we called a halt and talked the whole thing over. I fell in love with two of the dancing girls just by the horse sense they used in explaining to me the business of organization. One girl told me the theatre was like a factory. The people are like the wheels. If they don't all turn the same way at the same time they'll tear each other up.

I learnt a whole lot that first afternoon with the New Dance Group.

Sophie Maslow and me got together and I watched her play the talking machine and do the dances she had made up to a couple of my dust bowl songs. One was Dusty Old Dust and the other was I Aint Got No Home In This World Anymore.

With the record playing Sophie done a good job of dancing. I can't tell you how pretty and how nice Sophie is. That first day I had my suspicions that she was an awful good person—you know—one of the kind that works hard and likes everybody she sees.

Sophie's body looked so healthy and so active it looked like it would do almost anything she told it do. All she had to do was to notify it.

I watched her do her dances to my two Dust Bowl Ballads. I remember how I watched her feet. Dancers all have got a busted foot or ankle or back or shoulder or some certain mixture of it all. It's like a cowboy gets bow legs or like a cotton picker gets thorny hands. Yes—dancers have always got their troubles too. You can shake one's hand and always some other part of their body will fall off, a leg, an ear, their hair. I shook hands with one lady and her left hip dropped four inches. But I was all interested in Sophie's feet somehow that day.

I wondered how such a pretty woman could have such big feet. I don't know just how big they was but they seemed to spraddle out like and cover most of the floor. The floor was of white oak if it will help to clear your mind up any. I really don't think it will make much difference one way or the other because it is generally understood that most halls have got a floor. The only possible difference would be between some kind of a hard spruce or pine or oak. As I said this floor was white oak. It still is. And Sophie's feet are still as big—at least I had good reasons for thinking her feet covered the whole floor because she danced and brushed and scraped around so much that she really did cover the whole place.

She wore a little skirt—a long dress to rehearse in. She had a red looking hat she used to slap herself with and in this way to suggest how dusty it was in the dust bowl dances. The hall was so dirty and so dusty she didn't have to pretend much. It was as dusty and dirty as the dust bowl ever was.

After she got done with her dances she tried to teach me how to sing these same two songs like they was on the phonograph record. You'd be surprised how hard it is to sing a song the same way twice. Especially when you can't read music notes. I never could. I always just run my bluff, and sung them how I felt them.

But I'd come to the end of my rope. My jig was up. I'd been fooling the audience too long already, and now I fell in love with this whole gang of New Dancers and told them I would sing these songs for them. And one more song which another Almanac singer by the name of Lee Hays had put on a record—The Dodger.

I had to imitate Lee's voice in every way—not really imitate him—for I naturally have got my own way of singing. I don't sing out of books and neither does Lee very often. He's a boy from Arkansaw that's had a lot of hard luck piled on him and has got one of the best folk singing voices in the country. What I heard in Lee's voice was his tough luck. I liked the song but I found out that I had to also memorize and sing his song exactly like it was on the record. Lee had the asthma or bronchial trouble of some kind and he was under the doctor's care I knew on the day that he made this record. So he sung when he felt like it and he breathed and he rested and he paused when he felt like it. The outcome was that the record was all out of balance—not when you just listened to it in person—but—well—not— either—when you made up a dance to it. Because dancers like to dance to songs that are out of rhythm. It gives more dancers work. In other words if a song is just the same number of pauses and holds and the same rhythm all the way through it don't give a dancer much of a chance to show how good a dancer he is. But if a song ain't regular—that is—if it's different all of the way through with a different number of beats between each verse— then you see—this gives a dancer a chance to come out and do something new and different every time and it surprises you because it ain't the same every time—and you like it because it surprises you.

I was surprised when I seen the way the dancers danced this song The Dodger but I still desired and wanted to sing it for them. My only trouble was how to imitate Lee Hays' bronchial trouble and how to sing like I had his asthma and how to imagine all of this when I was physically in pretty good shape. How to rest and pause and how to take my breath as if I, too, had a case of bronchial trouble. No, I'm laughing at the very fact that I'd never had such a thing as this happen to me before. Oh I guess I've learned hundreds of songs off of records and then sung them in my own way but with the dancers I had to sing them so exact as to make it sound like the other singer felt on the day he made the record. To lots of trained musicians this wouldn't have been much of a trick but to a folk singer and an ear player like me—I'd always just sing like I felt—this was one of the hardest jobs I ever had to do.

The name of the dance is Sophie Maslow's Folksay which got such good reviews in some of the dance magazines and a couple of times in the New York Times. But these good reviews didn't grow like flowers. This young bunch of dancers worked their heads off practicing these dances that make up Folksay and then they worked their legs off and their arms—worked like dogs to teach me how to sing these folk songs with them."

Source

Woody Guthrie, "Singing, Dancing and Team-Work," 1942, published in Dave Marsh and Harold Leventhal, eds., *Pastures of Plenty: A Self-Portrait, Woody Guthrie.* New York: HarperCollins, 1990, 72–76.

LETTER FROM WOODY GUTHRIE TO ATTORNEY GENERAL TOM CLARK, JANUARY 12, 1949

Tom Clark was President Harry S. Truman's Attorney General. While the president was rather slow to fear the rise of domestic communism, Clark was more of a zealot, and launched a campaign to rid the country of those he believed to be subversives. He published a list of suspect organizations, past and present, and publicized his crusade a few years before Wisconsin Senator Joe McCarthy climbed on the Red Scare bandwagon. Woody here attacks Clark's encouragement of domestic paranoia, while the country has more serious problems, for which the answer is socialism. At that time, however, socialism (the government's heavy involvement in the economy) and communism (connected with the Soviet Union) were strongly linked, which is exactly what Woody is questioning. For Woody the disease is not communism, as Clark and his supporters would have it, but just the opposite, the fear of socialism/communism, and therefore anything on the left of the political spectrum. But Woody was swimming upstream, as the next few years would vividly demonstrate, when the Red Scare accelerated.

"Radio Station WNYC today is talking about the disease called cancer. Cancer is a disease that is partly caused by fear and kept aliving by other kinds of fears. It spreads in the tissues of nervous fear; it travels in the cell-towns of fears that rot out the nerves and highlines.

It can be started by fear. Planted with fear. Plowed and raised and seeded in the skylights of fear. The kinds of fear which keep cancer living and spreading, can and do keep other such diseases living and going. Like tuberculosis, venereal diseases, nervous diseases, heart diseases, bone diseases, ear eye nose and throat diseases, and I am asking you this morning to ask your own soul and conscience, sir, have you done anything to squirt any more poison of fear into the public bloodveins?

Have you caused anybody else to worry, to wonder, to be tricked, fooled, blinded, by the troubling fear that lives in the terrible jungle of worrying about your job. Worrying about low wages, worrying about high prices, fear about not being able to get into some kind of a better house and home?

Did you cause any living human anywhere on the face of the earth to take on any more bothersome, tiresome, terrible fears?

Fears about the war? Useless fears about another war on its bloody way to our streets and fields? Fears about the wild crazy use of our atom bomb? Fears about not being able to do the kind of work which every free person craves to do? Fears about not being able to make love, to get married, to breed and raise up a family, to house, to shelter, and to feed and clothe your family? Fears of losing everything you've been building up all of your life? Fears about taking down sick with no money to pay for medicine nor nurse nor doctor nor hospital? Fears about gambling and losing? Fears about empty stores, no customers and locked doors? Fears about no shipping, fears about no trading, fears about no freighting, no moving, no trucking, no loading, no jobs on the decks of our tied up rusty bottom boats and ships which stand still now because our big shots will not ship nor sell things to whole nations of people that they think along some line of body politics which you hate and fear?

What about the fears of the rise in the crime figures? Kids in their teens on the skids to the jails? Kids in their prime knocked out like broken lamps on account of not being able to find a chance to work, to be useful, to get paid, to have the joys of working, spending, shopping, and buying along the display windows? The use of splints, frames, and plaster casts cannot even touch within ten thousand miles, sir, of the real cause nor the real sure cure for the terrible lack of teachers, doctors, nurses, scientists, interns, students, in the fields of the healing arts and sciences.

There is only one cure for all of this, and that cure has already been found in millions of windows and streets around the world. That cure is socialized healing. Socialized medicine. Socialized living, socialized working, socialized thinking, and socialized resting, sleeping, seeding, breeding, which you may or may not be fearful about.

If you are full of fears about socialism, sir, then you are surely spreading your killing fears through your own self and through the whole civilized worlds; if you are trying to hold back this only certain cure for all of our hands and our brains (socialism), then you, you see are one of the causers and one of the spreaders of the fears that are causing all of the sickening diseases that already drown, choke, strangle, and kill the dreams, hopes, the plans, blueprints, and struggles, of the billion that now stagger sickly around and about."

Source

Woody Guthrie to Attorney General Tom Clark, January 12, 1949, published in Woody Guthrie, *Born To Win*, ed., Robert Shelton. New York: Collier Books, 1967, 65–68.

"Woody Guthrie: Hard Travellin'," an essay by Gordon Friesen

Gordon Friesen (1909–1996) had grown up in rural poverty in Oklahoma and moved to New York with his wife Agnes "Sis" Cunningham in 1941 to work with the Almanac Singers. Coming from a similar background, he and Woody became close friends. Gordon was a member of the Communist Party for many years, and while Woody never joined, they shared a similar political and social outlook, as well as a lifetime of living in poverty, and both were writers. In this sketch of Woody's life, published in 1963, Friesen presents a personal take on his friend's character, politics, and musical contributions. In 1962 Gordon and Sis launched *Broadside* magazine, devoted to the topical songs of Bob Dylan, Phil Ochs, Pete Seeger, Malvina Reynolds, Tom Paxton, and so many others. Gordon referred to the younger performers as "Woody's children."

"It was an unshakable belief in a brighter future for mankind that sustained Woody Guthrie during the drive of his creative career when conditions under which he worked, physical and otherwise, were often extremely difficult and harsh.

For him money was always very hard to come by, and he had many personal problems. Nevertheless, he managed besides considerable prose to write upwards of 1,000 songs (400 of which have been in the archives of the Library of Congress since the late '30's and are just now coming into circulation). Poverty crowded him at every step, as late as 1946 with the bulk of his best work behind him he was cutting the stencils and turning the mimeograph machine himself to put out a little songbook of his own and trying to make a few bucks by selling it around for 25¢ a copy. There were few takers.

Ironically, in this crude little hand-made booklet, covered with scrawled pleas for somebody to buy it, are some of the songs which in subsequent years have become nationally famous and have earned literally thousands of dollars. There is 'Hard Travelin'' and 'Biggest Thing' and 'This Land.' The latter is now his best known song. You can find it in countless songbooks, including those for America's school children who sing it as a patriotic hymn along with 'America The Beautiful.' 'This Land' has been recorded innumerable times; within the past six months or so alone it has appeared on no less than eight new L-P's, on such big labels as M-G-M, Warners, Columbia, Mercury, RCA-Victor, sung by such nationally popular artists as The Limeliters, Harry Belafonte Peter, Paul & Mary, the New Christy Minstrels, and so on.

This writer of course hasn't heard all the recordings made of 'This Land' or seen all the songbooks in which it has been printed. But he has yet to hear or see anywhere outside of Woody's little mimeographed book his final verse:

> 'Nobody living can ever stop me
> As I go walking my Freedom Highway
> Nobody living can make me turn back,
> This land is mde for you and me.'

During the year and a half Woody was with the Almanac Singers in New York City (1941–42) he wrote, in addition to a steady stream of songs, his autobiography 'Bound For Glory.' It is traditional for progressive artists in America to starve and freeze while working, and he did not escape this tradition. Most of the book was pounded out during icy winter nights in the unheated Almanac House on West 10th Street (there was hardly any money for food, let along a luxury like coal). He worked in the kitchen sitting on a wooden bench at his typewriter hunched down inside an old army coat several sizes too large for him. Coat collar turned up against his ears, he typed away. You could hear his machine gong all night long; when it stopped for a while you knew he had gotten up to warm his hands over the gas flame of the kitchen stove or refill his cup from the coffee pot with its thrice-used grounds. Many mornings you found him asleep by the typewriter, his head cradled in his arms on the table, with maybe 20 or 30 pages of new single-spaced, no margins copy piled beside him. As Woody says somewhere with his wry humor:

> 'Life is pretty tough. You're lucky if you live through it.'

His book, like many of his best songs, tells in stark detail of how hard things are for the 'little guy' in America. But Woody tells you one more very important thing: the days of tragedy and suffering are numbered; our train is 'bound for glory.'

In his writings and in his songs you can see his deep understanding of how this 'new world,' this, as he likes to call it, one big world 'union,' must come into being. It will not arrive automatically while you patiently wait for it at the station. First there is going to have to be considerable sacrifice and struggle. You do not wait for ideal conditions in which to work for it; you work wherever you are and struggle with whatever weapons you have. Woody's were his songs and writings and music. And Woody also has no illusions concerning on whose shoulders rests the main burden of bringing the better world about—it's going to have to be the ordinary guys[,] the workers in mines and mills and fields, the dispossessed, the unemployed, the racially persecuted—the 'humble people' as Fidel Castro calls them.

In the Almanac days Woody owned about one set of clothes— workingman's pants and shoes, a threadbare red-checkered flannel shirt, a sort of an 'Eisenhower jacket,' and the old army coat. He never wore hat or cap. He was in those days a thin, starved-looking guy, but fairly wiry. His black hair, always in need of cutting, was like a bramble bush, full of tight kinks which somebody described as 'the bobs from bob-wire.' He was quick to smile, but sometimes that smile hid seething emotions, although actual explosions of temper were rare. Among his mannerisms was a sort of disarming jauntiness; starting out on a booking he would sling his guitar across his back and stride along the street bent forward at the waist pretending that the instrument was a heavy load.

An old timer from the New York Unemployed Councils remembers a night in 1939 or '40 when Woody came up on the West Side of Manhattan to sing for his local. With Woody was a buddy, Mike Quin, the California writer who died of cancer in 1947. Woody sang and played for an hour or so, then collected his agreed-upon fee—75¢. He and Mike bought a bottle of wine and had enough money left over for the subway (those [were] the days of the nickel fare). On the way downtown Woody began singing and playing for the riders. Mike, who didn't have a bad Irish voice, joined in, and from among the passengers they picked up another singer. The trio wound up performing the whole night through, riding the subway out to the end of the line, New Lots Avenue, *and* back, out and back again, until past dawn....

It was only among the common people that Woody was really at home— among the unemployed, among subway riders, in union halls, in saloons across the land patronized by workers and drifters, in the camps of the migratory workers, on the Staten Island ferry, on merchant ships in World War II. There was little money to be found here; it was a world of nickels and dimes. The big money was in the world of commercial entertainment, but in order to share the loot you first had to sell your soul, and this Woody refused to do. The commercializers recognized his talent early and would undoubtedly have rewarded him liberally had he submitted to their wishes, broken his alliance with the people from whence he came, toned down and sugar-coated his criticism of society. There was a time when they saw him as potentially a second Will Rogers and launched a serious effort to shape him into one. But Woody, for much clearer reasons than motivated Holden Caulfield, walked out on the phonies. He found himself unable to endure, and finally rejected altogether the world of American bigtime entertainment populated, as he saw, by 'wheelers and dealers,' shifty-eyed, hypocritical, glib, fast-talking, sex-excited men and women who could not wake without benzedrine or go to sleep without barbiturates. Woody went instinctively back to the little people, who, although tainted by the corrupted, decaying society in which they live, do manage to hang onto an inner core of decency. He would leave a fruitless conference in some Rockefeller Center office where talk of fantastic sums of money flew all around, have a few beers, and go down with a buddy like Cisco Houston to sing and play on the Staten Island ferry, returning at 2 a.m. proud of his pocketful of coins with which the passengers had rewarded him.

By 1946 Woody was writing in the introduction of his mimeographed songbook:

> 'Several million skulls have been cracked while our human race has worked and fought its way up to the union. Do the big bands and orgasm gals sing a single solitary thing about that? No. Not a croak. Our spirit of work and sacrifice they cannot sing about because their brain is bought and paid for by the Big Money Boys who own and control them and hate our world union. They hate our real songs, our fight songs, our work songs, our union songs, because these are the Light of Truth and the mind of the racketeer cannot face the Light. I would not care so much how they choose to waste their personal lives but it is your money they are using to hide your own history from you and to make your future a worse one. Some day you will have a voice in how all your money is spent and then your songs will have some meaning.'

Much as he despised those in control of the entertainment field, Woody had even a greater hatred for the phonies in the progressive movement who mouthed radicalism as they compromised, adjusted and re-adjusted to the demands of Madison Avenue. Returning home one evening after tangling with a particularly obnoxious member of this breed, Woody smashed his mandolin against the wall, jumped up and down on the pieces, and it took several hours and a bottle of whiskey to calm him down.

As time went on it became increasingly more difficult for Woody to hide his true feelings. During the Almanac period, some well-meaning friend with connection would try to steer a few dollars their way by getting them an occasional booking at highclass society affairs. Woody would go along, and mink-coated bejeweled women would surround him, insulting him with every unwitting remark. 'Look, it's a real cowboy! Isn't he just darling—so picturesque.' One night at a high-powered affair in New York's Weston Hotel he shocked a penthouse full of cocktail drinking party goers by abruptly ripping down an expensive 20-foot brocaded drape, wrapping it around himself like an Indian and stalking out. (A diplomatic emissary from the hotel recovered the drape the next day.)

On another occasion a friend—probably the same misguided one—got Woody, Pete Seeger and Sis Cunningham a booking to sing in the Waldorf-Astoria for a nation convention of big business moguls of some kind or other—executives, managers, 'bosses.' It was the summer of 1942 and America was at war with the Hitler-Tojo fascists and fighting desperately to gain a toehlold in the Pacific. Pete [Seeger], then 22, was getting ready to leave for the Army in a few weeks.

The hour was fairly along when the three Almanacs stepped up to the microphone to 'entertain' their bosses. Much whiskey had already flowed down the throats of the four or five hundred conventioneers, eating hurriedly, impatient for the next promised round of pleasure—the girls. From some tables the cry was beginning to rise:

'Bring on the girls!'

The Almanacs sang a few of their new anti-fascist songs, but no one really listened; the drunken hub-bub drowned out their efforts. This time it was Pete's temper which exploded. He grabbed the mike and delivered a furious lecture which went something like this:

'What are you, human beings or a bunch of pigs! Here you sit slobbering whiskey, stuffing your fat bellies and hollerin for whores. Don't you care that American boys are dying tonight to save your country for you, and many more thousands will die before this is over. Great God Almighty, haven't you got any shame.!'

Frankly, it was like shouting against the wind; a drunk millionaires at one of the front table bawled: 'Aw, shut up, and play some music. How about 'She'll Be Comin' Around the Mountain'.'

Woody's guitar and Sis' accordion took up the song, and Pete cooled off by concentrating on the strings of his long-necked banjo. After a few minutes, Woody said:

'Let me take the next verse.'

Stepping real close to the microphone so that the room was filled with the sound of his voice, he sang to the bosses:

'She'll be wearin' a union button when she comes,
She'll be wearin' a union button when she comes,
She'll be wearin' a union button,
She'll be wearing' a union button,
She'll be wearing' a union button when she comes.'

When he finished there was a moment of hush, in which Woody, Pete and Sis packed up their instruments and walked off the sage; but as they left, the drunken cry rose again, louder than ever:

'Bring on the girls! Bring on the girls!'

Various people 'discovered' Woody Guthrie early in his active career. But it was Mike Quinn, then writing his column for the People's Daily *World* on the West Coast, who probably discovered him first. Woody had a radio program on a small California station singing an hour or two each day in return for whatever change he could coax out of his listeners by mail by selling them mimeographed copies of the songs (he had to mimeograph them himself). He began by singing 'country music,' the traditional songs he learned back in Oklahoma and Texas. Many of these were what are known as 'white spirituals' of a passive religious 'pie in the sky' nature. The composers agreed that conditions here on earth are intolerable for poor folks, but there is nothing you can do about it except wail and grieve. You must quietly and submissively bear your burden of misery and pain and wait hopefully for the release of death, when you will fly up to happier surroundings. So following this tradition into the '30's we even had songs to the effect that 'There's No Depression in Heaven.'

Somewhere along the line Woody rebelled at endlessly singing this sort of wailing defeatism. He took a song called 'I Ain't Got No Home In This World Anymore' and rewrote the lyrics. In Woody's new words it is *not* inscrutable fate which takes your home away; your home is deliberately stolen from you by greedy bankers, landlords and other earthly rats 'who will rob you with a fountain pen.' His 'Okie' and "Arky' listeners who had flooded into California as 'dust bowl refugees' ate it up, and soon he was re-writing other songs and starting to compose new ones in the same vein.

Mike Quin heard Woody, came by to meet him, and they became good friends. Woody treasured Mike's writings and they undoubtedly were a main inspiration for him from then on. If you read Mike's collected work 'On The Drumhead' along with Woody's songs and prose you will see many of the same things. Both men are filled with a tremendous love for humanity, share a deep identification with the underdog, an intense hatred of injustice, a wry but biting sense of humor, and, above all a mutual determination to do their part to make this a better world.

The work of each shows a very special feeling for the mistreatment and suffering of oppressed minorities. The exploited 'Mexican Hands' Mike saw being deported from the California fields in 1933 reappear on a doomed plane 15 years after in Woody's song 'The Deportees.' (Is this the only name we can give them after their long labors to load our tables with food and wine, Woody asks, and then rights this wrong by giving them names himself in a beautiful chorus).

Both came from similarly impoverished and bitter backgrounds, Mike from the slums of San Francisco, Woody from the ravished dust bowl. (They even resembled each other physically, both being of medium height, thin, with heads of curly hair, high foreheads, sharpish noses and chins, with eyes that had seen an awful lot of hunger, misery and death).

It might be interesting to compare the work of one of 'Woody's Children,' today's young Bob Dylan, with that of Mike Quin, of whom Bob has probably never heard. Take these lines from one of Mike's anti-war poems:

'Another crimson flood,
Another ship you'd launch upon our blood—
A toast you'd drink with wine that has been crushed
From mangled bodies lying in the mud.'

Then consider these lines from Dylan's already almost classic song 'Masters of War' (written in 1963 and published in *Broadside* #20):

'You fasten the triggers for others to fire,
Then you sit back as the death count gets higher,
You hide in your mansions as the young people's blood
Flows out of their bodies and is buried in the mud.'

A love of life, a tenacious determination to cling to every precious second of it, this Mike had and Woody has. In a piece written after his doctors told him he had only about two months to live, Mike wrote: 'I intend to live as fully as possible to the last sweet moment.' One of the great difficulties in writing about Woody is that one falls without wishing to into the use of the past tense. It has been some eight years now since his creative career ended when he was hospitalized with Huntington's Chorea, an insidious disease of slow but seemingly irreversible muscular disintegration believed to be hereditary. No cure for it is known, but Woody has fought it eery inch of the way these long years. As his wife, Marjorie, wrote in a letter last spring: 'Woody is slowly deteriorating but fighting hard to "stay around," in spite of the fact that he can barely stand, eat, dress himself, etc.' And in a more recent letter to his friends: 'He looks like he is about to fall any minute … but he remains standing. To see him light a cigarette is really to see a man fighting for his life. Yes, he wants to live!'

Huntington's Chorea is considered incurable. Yet who knows what a bit of intense research might turn up. It might not cost more than one hydrogen bomb, or even one nuclear submarine."

Source

Gordon Friesen, "Woody Guthrie: Hard Travellin'," *Mainstream*, vol. 16, no. 8, August 1963, 4-11.

"Woodrow Wilson Guthrie (1912–1967),"
an essay by John Greenway

John Greenway (1919–1991) had degrees in English and Anthropology, taught at the University of Colorado, and published 19 books, including the ground-breaking *American Folk Songs of Protest* (1953). His left-wing politics early drew him to Woody, but in the 1960s he became increasingly more politically conservative. In this obituary of Guthrie, Greenway maintains his long standing praise, yet also condemns his radical songs as well as his careless, shiftless lifestyle. Greenway assumes that many of his songs will survive in popular culture, with the emphasis on the "good and simple" patriot as expressed in "This Land Is Your Land." He believes, indeed hopes, that his radical politics will soon be forgotten. This is an important interpretation that captures the complexities of Woody's life and public image written just after his death. His papers are now readily available in the Woody Guthrie Archives, Mt. Kisco, New York, as well as in the American Folklife Center of the Library of Congress, and the Ralph Rinzler Folklife Archives and Collections, Smithsonian Center for Folklife and Cultural Heritage in Washington, D.C.

———————

"On the third of October death came for Woody Guthrie, a mercy delayed for the full term of 13.7 years allotted Huntington's choreics between the onset of their disease and its fatal termination. Now being the legend of Woody Guthrie.

It will be a legendary process of compelling interest for us. As students of past legend[a]ry, we are not often privileged to observe mythopoetic forces beginning their work of creation. It is even more rare to have one of our own become legend. And since no group of persons outside our Society know so well and so dispassionately both Guthrie and the forces remolding him, we have a responsibility to attend upon the process, for there are no others to hold the truth of Guthrie above the other considerations working upon his image.

There are already two legendary Guthries. One was made out of innocent necessity by the popular press, building a foundation upon that most useless of hypocrisies, *de mortuis nil nisi bonum*. Woody Guthrie in McLuhanland is a good and simple man who brightly sang his sound of music through the agonies of the Dust Bowl Exodus and the Great Depression like an unwanted child of the Trapp Family. But how else could the mass media equate the real Guthrie with the man who composed what is perhaps the greatest affirmation of America yet put into song?

The other Guthrie is darker in visage and longer in the making. This is Woody Guthrie Hero of the Proletariat, long needed to fill the place of that first shaker of singing fists who died by the bullets of Utah's firing squad in 1915. [Joe] Hill's factitious legend was kept alive as long as determination could help it, but when he said 'I never died,' it was just the last of his lies.

If he had never written his songs, Guthrie's life would be only an exercise in the banality of tragedy. He was born in the boom town of Okemah, Oklahoma, in the year Woodrow Wilson became President. His father courted and won ineffectuality—he had arthritis, but he became a pugilist; he was a Socialist, but he became a real estate speculator. Woody's mother was a beautiful woman—until that dread insanity of the muscles burst out of its latent heredity. 'I used to go to sleep at night and have dreams,' Woody wrote in his great autobiography, *Bound for Glory*; 'I dreamed that my mama was just like anybody else. I saw her talking, smiling, and working just like other kids' mamas. But when I woke up it would still be all wrong.'

Fires pursued Woody throughout his life. Two of them destroyed his homes in childhood; another burned his sister to death; and a last fiery tragedy sent his mother to the insane asylum and his badly burned father into terminal apathy. Woody and his brother Roy were left alone in their family's decayed two-room shanty, orphans of living parents. Woody took to the road, and that was his real home for the rest of his active life. He had talents, but his feet were too fast for his hands. When he had work, he was a hobo; when he was idle, he was a tramp. He married—once, twice, three times? He had children—two, three more? One was burned to death in an electrical fire during her parents' absence. But neither wives nor children could keep him from his compulsive, aimless rambling.

At the end of America's Red Decade he drifted into New York, drawn by that strange centripetal force that brought together such disparate rebels as Aunt Molly Jackson from the coal mines of Kentucky and Pete Seeger from the classrooms of Harvard. There they hammered folksongs into weapons of subversion. There were others far more sophisticated and intelligent than Guthrie and they persuaded him that bad luck was a byproduct of capitalism. He was a victim of deceit, but he was a willing victim, and he led others into the same entrapment. He composed a dozen execrable songs to help Howard Fast lure thousands of dupes up to Peekskill, New York, to have their heads broken in the glorious cause of Communism. Gurhrie also wrote a regular column for two Communist newspapers in which he explicitly advocated the composition of songs to fan the flames of discontent. But he was only a limp leftist at best a born deviationist, and those in his group who remain to this day ever faithful to political infidelity condemned his work until fourteen years ago, when he nearly burned off his hand in a gasoline fire and entered the hospital for his long wait for death. Then he became useful to them and worthy of the apotheosis they are conferring upon him with their legend.

Legend-making begins with the breaking of paradoxes into simplicities. Next, the useful simplicities are built into a structure that surrounds the real man as a scaffold surrounds a great statue. But unlike art, legend[a]ry breaks the statue away and leaves the scaffolding to represent reality.

But what is reality in Woody Guthrie? Among the 1,400 songs he claimed to have written only ten per cent are songs of protest, yet these are the whole for the image of the proletarian hero. He also wrote songs of quite unprintable obscenity, but no myth-makers have as yet seen any use for them. In both the world of McLuhan and the world of Lenin obituaries have recalled his hatred of a 'song that makes you think that you're not any good,' but no one else ever wrote songs of such venomous scurrility against people he did not like. His songs of protest scorch the irresponsibility of cops and capitalists, yet he was a man of monumental personal irresponsibility. His indictment of those who would 'rob you with a fountain pen' will live as long as his legend, but as visitor to your home he would walk off with your guitar or you wife with equal want and willingness. He could write songs as infernally bad as 'Kloo Klacka Klambo' and as supernally good as 'Deportees.' He was well enough read in revolutionary literature to write paeans to Gerhard Eisler, yet he never left the folk.

Scholarship might resolve some of these paradoxes if the existent documents were available, but they are not. Some of Guthrie's songs, letters, and other writings are in the hands of a dubious group called the 'Guthrie Children's Fund,' who let no one outside their own purposes see them. The rest are in the possession of his antepenultimate-penultimate wife, who guards them with equal fervor.

If fear has any place in their motivation, these people are fearing without cause. Guthrie is as safe from his writings as Jesus Christ is safe from the Dead Sea Scrolls. What will matter after all of us are gone is what the culture chooses to matter, and that will be the truth for our culture. There is no doubt that Guthrie the proletarian hero will vanish as certainly as Joe Hill. What will endure are a handful of magnificent songs—the songs of the Dust Bowl, the songs that children grow on, the songs that school-children of the Pacific Northwest sing about the dams at Bonneville and the Grand Coulee and the song that all America will sing long beyond our memory, 'This Land Is Your Land.' And since these will endure, their composer will endure, and he will be the man he must have been to write them."

Source

John Greenway, "Woodrow Wilson Guthrie (1912–1967)," *Journal of American Folklore*, vol. 81, no. 319, Jan.–Mar. 1968, 62–64.

Notes

Introduction

1 "This Land Is Your Land," Harold Leventhal & Marjorie Guthrie, eds., *The Woody Guthrie Songbook* (New York: Grosset & Dunlap, 1976), 225.

Chapter 1

1. Dave Marsh and Harold Leventhal, eds., *Pastures of Plenty: A Self-Portrait, Woody Guthrie* (New York: HarperCollins, 1990), 3.
2. Marsh and Leventhal, eds., *Pastures of Plenty*, 4.
3. Marsh and Leventhal, eds., *Pastures of Plenty*, 5; Woody Guthrie, *Bound For Glory* (New York: E. P. Dutton & Co., 1943), 226.
4. Marsh and Leventhal, eds., *Pastures of Plenty*, 5.
5. Marsh and Leventhal, eds., *Pastures of Plenty*, 5-6.
6. Marsh and Leventhal, eds., *Pastures of Plenty*, 6; Woody Guthrie, "A Few Kind Words Prepared For Miss Mary Ann Guthrie," February 5, 1937, Thelma Bray, *Reflections: The Life and Times of Woody Guthrie* (Pampa: Thelma Bray, 2002), 5-6.
7. Robert S. Koppelman, ed., *"Sing Out, Warning! Sing Out, Love!": The Writings of Lee Hays* (Amherst: University of Massachusetts Press, 2003), 166.
8. Marsh and Leventhal, eds., *Pastures of Plenty*, 7.
9. Marsh and Leventhal, eds., *Pastures of Plenty*, 7.
10. Ed Robbin, *Woody Guthrie and Me* (Berkeley: Lancaster-Miller Publishers, 1939), 35.
11. Mary Jo Guthrie Edgmon, *My Favorite Things About My Brother, Woody Guthrie* (Oklahoma Historical Society, 2002), 5.
12. Robbin, *Woody Guthrie and Me*, 41.
13. Robbin, *Woody Guthrie and Me*, 108; Marsh and Leventhal, eds., *Pastures of Plenty*, 7. Geer would later make his reputation as the character Grandpa Walton on the popular CBS TV show *The Waltons*, 1972–1978.
14. Marsh and Leventhal, eds., *Pastures of Plenty*, 8.
15. Robbin, *Woody Guthrie and Me*, 112.

16. Pete Seeger with Robert Santelli, "Hobo's Lullaby," in *Hard Travelin'.: The Life and Legacy of Woody Guthrie*, ed. Robert Santelli and Emily Davidson (Hanover and London, 1999), 22–23.

17. Koppelman, ed., "*Sing Out, Warning! Sing Out, Love!*", 163.

18. Robbin, *Woody Guthrie and Me*, 115; "'Geer, Woody, in Anti-War Songs Tonight," *Sunday Worker*, November 10, 1940, 7.

19. Alan Lomax, Woody Guthrie, Pete Seeger, *Hard Hitting Songs for Hard-Hit People* (New York: Oak Publications, 1967), 362.

20. *It Shall Not Come To Pass*, sheet music published by TAC Radio Division, with no publisher or date.

21. Marsh and Leventhal, eds., *Pastures of Plenty*, 9; Alan Lomax, "Introductory Comments," *Woody Guthrie Library of Congress Recordings*, Elektra Records EKL 217/272, 1964, liner notes.

22. "Alan Lomax," Judah L. Graubart and Alice V. Graubart, *Decade of Destiny* (Chicago: Contemporary Books, 1978), 318.

23. Henrietta Yurchenco assisted by Marjorie Guthrie, *A Mighty Hard Road: The woody Guthrie Story* (New York: McGraw-Hill Book Co., 1970), 9–11.

24. Henrietta Yurchenco, *Around the World in 80 Years: A Memoir* (Port Richmond, CA: MRI Press, 2002), 39; Gene Marine, "Guerrilla Minstrel," *Rolling Stone*, issue 106, April 13, 1972, 42.

25. Lomax, Guthrie, Seeger, *Hard Hitting Songs for Hard-Hit People*, 15, 25.

26. Marsh and Leventhal, eds., *Pastures of Plenty*, 9; Jeffrey Pepper Rodgers, "Pete Seeger: How Can I Keep from Singing?," *Acoustic Guitar*, vol. 13, no. 1, July 2002, 56.

27. Alan Lomax to Woody Guthrie, November 1, 1940, Ronald D. Cohen, ed., *Alan Lomax, Assistant in Charge: The Library of Congress Letters, 1935–1945* (Jackson: University Press of Mississippi, 2011), 189.

28. Woody Guthrie to Will, Herta, and Kate, February 27, 1941, in Woody Guthrie Archives, Correspondence 1, Box 1, Folder 18; Woody Guthrie, *Woody Sez* (New York: Grosset & Dunlap, 1975), 132; Alan Lomax to Charles Todd, March 17, 1941, Cohen, ed., *Alan Lomax, Assistant in Charge*, 214.

29. Dave Johnson, "… just a mile from the end of the line," *Northwest Magazine*, February 2, 1969, 10.

30. Marsh and Leventhal, eds., *Pastures of Plenty*, 9–10; Cohen, ed., *Alan Lomax, Assistant in Charge*, 265.

31. Bess Lomax, *Sing It Pretty: A Memoir* (Urbana: University of Illinois Press, 2008), 40.

32. Marsh and Leventhal, eds., *Pastures of Plenty*, 10.

33. Agnes "Sis" Cunningham and Gordon Friesen, *Red Dust and Broadsides: A Joint Autobiography* (Amherst: University of Massachusetts Press, 1999), 207, 211; Marsh and Leventhal, eds., *Pastures of Plenty*, 10.

34. Guthrie, *Woody Sez*, 127.

35. David King Dunaway and Molly Beer, *Singing Out: An Oral History of America's Folk Music Revivals* (New York: Oxford University Press, 2010), 54; Marsh and Leventhal, eds., *Pastures of Plenty*, 106.

36. "Out of the People's World-Wide Fight Against the Axis comes This New Music: A Folk Festival to Be Heard at Town Hall Tomorrow Night," *Daily Worker*, June 25, 1942; Earl Robinson with Eric Gordon, *Ballad Of An American: The Autobiography of Earl Robinson* (Lanham, MD: The Scarecrow Press, 1998), 141.

37. Cunningham and Friesen, *Red Dust and Broadsides*, 223–224; Cohen, ed., *Alan Lomax, Assistant in Charge*, 314.

38. Kenneth C. Kaufman, "Another Literary Black Eye for Oklahoma," *The Daily Oklahoman*, March 21, 1943; Clifton Fadiman, *The New Yorker*, March 20, 1943, 68.

39. Marsh and Leventhal, eds., *Pastures of Plenty*, 11; Jim Longhi, *Woody, Cisco and Me: Seamen Three in the Merchant Marine* (Urbana: University of Illinois Press, 1997), 2.

40 Longhi, *Woody, Cisco and Me*, 38, 54–55.

41. Moses Asch, "The Ballad of Chanukah," *Sing Out!*, vol. 17 no. 6, Deember/January 1967/68, 12.

42. Marsh and Leventhal, eds., *Pastures of Plenty*, 11.

CHAPTER 2

1. Dave Marsh and Harold Leventhal, eds., *Pastures of Plenty: A Self-Portrait, Woody Guthrie* (N.Y.: HarperCollins, 1990), 13–14.

2. "Editorials," *Christian Science Monitor*, Mar 4, 1947.

3. Marsh and Leventhal, eds., *Pastures of Plenty*, 197, 199–200.

4. Liner Notes, *Woody Guthrie: Songs to Grow on For Mother and Child*, Smithsonian Folkways CD SF 45035, 1991; Beatrice Landeck, "Introduction," *Songs To Grow On: Nursery Days*, Folkways Records FC 7675, 1951; Earl Robinson with Eric Gordon, *Ballad of an American: The Autobiography of Earl Robinson* (Lanham, MD: The Scarecrow Press, 1998), 147.

5. Marsh and Leventhal, eds., *Pastures of Plenty*, 178.

6. Pete Seeger, "Woody Guthrie," *People's Songs*, vol. 2, No. 7 and 7, July and August 1947, 18; liner notes, *Dust Bowl Ballads*, Folkways Records FH 5212, 1964 (previously *Ballads From the Dust Bowl*); Henrietta Yurchenco assisted by Marjorie Guthrie, *A Mighty Hard Road: The Woody Guthrie Story* (New York: McGraw-Hill Book Co., 1970), 127.

7. Marsh and Leventhal, eds., *Pastures of Plenty*, 202.

8. Marsh and Leventhal, eds., *Pastures of Plenty*, 89; Irma and Mordecai Bauman, *From Our Angle of Repose: A Memoir* (New York: Privately Printed, 2006), 283.

9. Marsh and Leventhal, eds., *Pastures of Plenty*, 185.

10. Charles Seeger, "Reviews," *Journal of American Folklore*, vol. 61, April–June 1948, 217.

11. Robert S. Koppelman, ed., *"Sing Out, Warning! Sing Out, Love!": The Writings of Lee Hays* (Amherst: University of Massachusetts Press, 2003), 155.

12. Harold Leventhal, "Foreword," Marsh and Leventhal, eds., *Pastures of Plenty*, xiii; Harold Leventhal with Robert Santelli, "Remembering Woody," Robert Santelli and Emily Davidson, eds., *Hard Travelin': The Life and Legacy of Woody Guthrie* (Hanover: Wesleyan University Press, 1999), 15; Koppelman, ed., *"Sing Out, Warning! Sing Out, Love!"*, 152.

13. Pete Seeger with Robert Santelli, "Hobo's Lullaby," Santelli and Davidson, eds., *Hard Travelin'*, 31–32.

14. Woody Guthrie, "Foreword," Jonny Whiteside, *Ramblin' Rose: The Life and Career of Rose Maddox* (Nashville: Country Music Foundation Press, 1997), xi, xiii.

15. Woody Guthrie, "Folk-Songs—'Non-Politickled' Pink," *Sing Out!*, vol. 2, no. 11, May 1952, 10.

16. Woody Guthrie, "I've Got To Know," *Sing Out!*, vol. 1, no. 6, October 1950, 14; "A Letter From Woody Guthrie," *ibid.* vol. 2, no. 3, September 1951, 2, 14; Woody Guthrie, "Folk-Songs—'Non-Politickled' Pink," ibid., vol. 2, no. 11, May 1952, 10.

17. Erik Darling, *"I'd Give My Life": From Washington Square to Carnegie Hall: A Journey by Folk Music* (Palo Alto, CA: Science and Behavior Books, 2008), 17, 29.

18. Elliott quoted in Hank Reineke, *Ramblin' Jack Elliott: The Never-Ending Highway* (Lanham, MD: The Scarecrow Press, 2010), 39.

19. Bill Stamm, "Woody Guthrie—the man and the music," *Jazz Music*, vol. 8, No. 5, Sept./Oct. 1957, 5.

20. Woody Guthrie to Ken Lindsay, February 25, 1952, Lindsay to Guthrie, September 23, 1952 (ellipses in original), "Ken Lindsay Collection of Woody Guthrie Correspondence," American Folklife Center, Library of Congress, Washington, D.C., AFC 2005/006.

21. Ed Robbin, *Woody Guthrie and Me* (Berkeley: Lancaster-Miller Publishers, 1979), 116.

22. Woody Guthrie to Ken Lindsay, September 16, 1953, "Ken Lindsay Collection of Woody Guthrie Correspondence," American Folklife Center.
23. "John Cohen II," Ronald D. Cohen, ed., *Wasn't That A Time!*: *Firsthand Accounts of the Folk Music Revival* (Lanham, Md: The Scarecrow Press, 1995), 182.
24. "Heritage: U.S.A.," *Sing Out!*, vol. 2, no. 5 (November 1951), 8.
25. John Greenway, *American Folksongs of Protest* (Philadelphia: University of Pennsylvania Press, 1953), 277, 282; Russell Ames, *The Story of American Folk Song* (New York: Grosset & Dunlap, 1955), 275.
26. "The Kids Write To Woody," *Sing Out!*, vol. 5, no. 4, Autumn 1955, 34; "Woody Guthrie," *ibid.*, vol. 6, no. 2, Spring 1956, 35.
27. Pete Seeger, "Johnny Appleseed, Jr.," *Sing Out!*, vol. 7, no. 3, Fall 1957, 32.
28. *Bound For Glory: The Songs and Story of Woody Guthrie*, Folkways Records FP 78/1, 1956, booklet.
29. "This record made me cry, says Jack Elliott," *Melody Maker*, December 13, 1958, 15; John Greenway, "Folk Song Discography," *Western Folklore*, vol. xx, no. 2, April 1961, 151.
30. Pete Seeger, "An Introductory Note About The Man And His Music," Woody Guthrie, *California to the New York Island* (New York: The Guthrie Children's Trust Fund, 1958), 5.
31. Pete Seeger, "Woody Guthrie: Lessons he taught us," *Caravan*, no. 16, April-May 1959), 14–15.
32. John Greenway, *Talking Blues*, Folkways Records FH 5232, 1958, liner notes.
33. Alex Kochanoff, "Woody Guthrie," *Gardyloo*, no. 5, September 1959, 7.
34. *The Woody Guthrie Newsletter*, no. 1, April 1960, [4].
35. Robert Smith, "Woody Guthrie today," *Melody Maker*, June 11, 1960, 5; Smith, "Woody Guthrie today," *Melody Maker*, June 18, 1960, 4.
36. *The Woody Guthrie Newsletter*, no. 1, April 1960, [2].

CHAPTER 3

1. Pete Seeger, "Why Folk Music?," David A. DeTurk and A. Poulin, Jr., eds., *The American Folk Scene* (New York: Dell Publishing Co., 1967), 48.
2. "Folk Concerts Jazz Up B. O. [Box Office]," *Variety*, February 26, 1958, 43.
3. Robert Shelton, "A Man To Remember: Woody Guthrie," *Woody Guthrie: Library of Congress Recordings*, Elektra Records EKL-271/272, 1964, liner notes.
4. "Jon Pankake," Ronald D. Cohen, ed., *Wasn't That A Time!*: *Firsthand Accounts of the Folk Music Revival* (Lanham, Md.: The Scarecrow Press, 1995), 111.
5. *The Little Sandy Review*, no. 5, 34, 37.
6. "John Greenway On Woody Guthrie," *The Little Sandy Review*, no. 9, 40, 42.
7. Alan Lomax, *The Folk Songs of North America* (New York: Doubleday & Company, 1960), 426.
8. Oscar Brand, "Woodrow Wilson Guthrie: Writer," *Disc Collector*, no. 16, 5.
9. Logan English, "Woody Guthrie," *Disc Collector*, no. 16, 15.
10. *Cisco Houston sings the songs of Woody Guthrie*, Vanguard Records VRS-9089, 1961, liner notes; Woody Guthrie, "Cisco Houston," *900 Miles: the Ballads, Blues and Folksongs of Cisco Houston* (New York: Oak Publications, 1965), Robert Shelton, "Novel Way to Teach," *New York Times*, May 14, 1961.
11. Henrietta Yurchenco assisted by Marjorie Guthrie, *A Mighty Hard Road: The Woody Guthrie Story* (New York: McGraw-Hill Book Co., 1970), 144.
12. Dylan postcard quoted in Howard Sounes, *Down the Highway: The Life of Bob Dylan* (New York: Grove Press, 2001), 78–79; Review of *Bob Dylan*, *The Little Sandy Review*, no. 22, 15, 18.
13. Bob Dylan, *Chronicles: Volume One* (New York: Simon & Schuster, 2004), 98, 82–83.

14. Liner notes, *Folkways: A Vision Shared: A Tribute to Woody Guthrie and Leadbelly,* CBS Records C44034, 1988.

15. "Jack Elliott: (Woody Guthrie's) Songs to Grow On," *The Little Sandy Review,* no. 18, 8.

16. John Greenway, "Notes," *jack elliott sings the songs of woody guthrie,* Prestige Folklore 14011, 1961; Pete Welding, "Folk Music Round-Up," *Sing Out!,* vol. 11, no. 5, Dec.-Jan. 1961-62, 59; "Jack Elliott Sings The Songs Of Woody Guthrie," *The Little Sandy Review,* no. 16, 31, 33.

17. Elliott quoted in Robert Shelton, *No Direction Home: The Life and Music of Bob Dylan* (New York: William Morrow, 1986), 101–102; Suze Rotolo, *A Freewheelin' Time: A Memoir of Greenwich Village in the Sixties* (New York: Broadway Books, 2008), 125–126; Elliott quoted in Sounes, *Down the Highway,* 88.

18. Agnes "Sis" Cunningham and Gordon Friesen, *Red Dust and Broadsides: A Joint Autobiography* (Amherst: University of Massachusetts Press, 1999), 291, 292; Gordon Friesen, "Songs For Our Time," *Mainstream,* vol. 15, no. 12, December 1962, 7.

19. Gordon Friesen, "Introduction," Sis Cunningham, ed., *Broadside: Songs of our ties from the pages of Broadside Magazine, Volume 1* (New York: A Oak Publications, 1964), 10; David Dunaway and Molly Beer, *Singing Out: An Oral History of America's Folk Music Revivals* (New York: Oxford University Press, 2010), 161–162.

20. Pete Seeger, "Introduction," *Woody Guthrie Folk Songs* (New York: Ludlow Music, Inc., 1963), 6.

21. Bess Hawes, "View of Woody Guthrie," *Broadside* (Los Angeles), #2, April 1962, 1–2.

22. Robert Shelton, "Introduction," *Born To Win: Woody Guthrie* (New York: Collier Books, 1965), 14; Jack Elliott, "Woody Guthrie Revisited," *Sing Out!,* vol. 15, no. 6, January 1966, 79; Miles Beardslee, "Book Review," Rag Baby, vol. 1, no. 2, October 1965.

23. "Leisure: String 'Em Up," *Time,* January 5, 1962, 46

24. Pete Seeger, "Six New Songs By Woody Guthrie," *Sing Out!,* vol. 13, no 1, February-March 1963, 9.

25. Alfred Hendricks, "Woody Guthrie In Hospital For 10 Years," *New York Post,* March 4, 1963, 85; Peter Seeger, "Remembering Woody," *Mainstream,* vol. 16, no. 8, August 1963, 31; Phil Ochs, "The Guthrie Legacy," ibid., 34–35.

26. Josh Dunson, *Freedom In The Air: Song Movements Of The 60's* (New York: International Publishers, 1965), 45–46.

27. Robert Shelton, "Guthrie's Heirs," *New York Times,* June 14, 1964.

28. Ernie Marrs, "The Incompleat Woody," *Broadside,* #40, February 25, 1964; John Greenway, "The Anatomy of a Genius: Woody Guthrie," *Hootenanny,* vol. 1, no. 3, May 1964, 17.

29. John Greenway, "Woody Guthrie: The Man, the Land, the Understanding," *The American West,* vol. 3, no. 4 (1966), reprinted in De Turk and Poulin, *The American Folk Scene,* 199.

30. Gordon Friesen, "Calling Dr. Greenway," *Broadside,* #46, May 30, 1964.

31. Logan English, "For The Good He Taught, And The Dignity He Gave Us," *Folk Music,* August 1964, 52–53.

32. Peter Welding, Liner Notes, *Dust Bowl Ballads: Woody Guthrie,* RCA Victor LPV-502.

33. Shelton, "A Man To Remember: Woody Guthrie," *Woody Guthrie: Library of Congress Recordings*; John Dunson, "To Know the Man," *Broadside,* #53, December 20, 1964.

34. D. K. Wilgus, "Woody Guthrie," *The Journal of American Folklore,* vol. 80, no. 316, Apr.–Jun. 1967), 204.

35. Robert Shelton, "Guthrie Honored By Folk Concert," *New York Times,* April 19, 1965.

36. Yurchenco, *A Mighty Hard Road,* 149; Pete Seeger with Robert Santelli, "Hobo's Lullaby," Robert Santelli and Emily Davidson, eds., *Hard Travelin': The Life and Legacy of Woody Guthrie* (Hanover: Wesleyan University Press, 1999), 32–33.

37. Jean Heller, "Guthrie's Songs Catch On—But It's Too Late," *Los Angeles Times,* March 4, 1966, 20.

38. Letter from Stewart Udall quoted in *Stray Notes from the Atlanta Folk Music Society,* vol.

1, no. 12, May 1, 1966; Robert B. Semple, *New York Times,* April 7, 1966, 45; Harold Leventhal, "Foreword," Dave Marsh and Harold Leventhal, eds., *Pastures of Plenty: A Self-Portrait, Woody Guthrie* (New York: HarperCollins, 1990), xiii.

39. Leventhal, "Foreword," Marsh and Leventhal, eds., *Pastures of Plenty,* xiii; Moses Asch, Liner Notes, *Woody Guthrie Bonneville Dam & Other Columbia River Songs,* Verve/Folkways FV-9036.

40. John Cashman, "Folk Hero," *New York Post,* April 19, 1966, 27; Michael Iachetta, "The Saga of Woody Guthrie," *New York Sunday News,* May 1, 1966, Section II, 1s.

41. Editor's note, Camilla Adams, "Woody Guthrie In The Days Of The Almanac Singers," *Broadside,* #71, June 1966, 7; Irwin Silber, "Fan the Flames," *Sing Out!,* vol. 17, no. 6, December-January 1967/68, 55.

42. Dave Johnson, "… just a mile from the end of the line," *Northwest Magazine,* February 2, 1969, 11.

43. Dorian Keyser, "Woody Guthrie Still Top Draw," *Songmakers Newsletter,* vol. 1, no. 6, Oct. 1967; Jean White, "Will Geer finds it good living in the muddy stream of history," *Boston Globe TV Week Section,* January 6, 1974, 13.

44. Harold Leventhal with Robert Santelli, "Remembering Woody," Santelli and Davidson, eds., *Hard Travelin',* 20; Seeger with Santelli, "Hobo's Lullaby," ibid., 33.

45. Leventhal with Santelli, "Remembering Woody," Santelli and Davidson, eds., *Hard Travelin',* 21.

CHAPTER 4

1. "Woody Guthrie, Folk Singer and Composer, Dies," *New York Times,* October 4, 1967, 47; Phil Casey, "Woody Guthrie Dies of Muscular Illness; Wrote Songs, Sang About Poor People," *Washington Post,* October 4, 1967 B6.

2. Arlo Guthrie, "Despite The Shadow of his Father's (and Possily his Own) Deadly Disease, a Folk Hero Celebrates LIfe," *People Weekly,* vol. 18, no. 10, September 7, 1987.

3. Pete Seeger, "So Long, Woody, It's Been Good To Know Yu," *LIfe,* November 10, 1967, 8; Pete Seeger, "So Long, Woody, It's Been Good To Know Ya," Woody Guthrie, *Bound For Glory* (New York: New American Library, 1970), viii.

4. Irwin Silber, "Fan The Flames," *Sing Out!,* vol. 17, no. 6, December/January 1967/68, 54; Irwin Silber, "Woodie [sic] Guthrie: He Never Sold Out," *National Guardian,* October 14, 1967, 10.

5. Robert S. Koppelman, ed., *"Sing Out, Warning! Sing Out, Love!": The Writings of Lee Hays* (Amherst: University of Massachusetts Press, 2003), 156, 204.

6. "Woodrow Wilson Guthrie (1912–1967)," *Broadside,* #85, October 1967.

7. Ralph J. Gleason, "The Strong Songs of Woody Guthrie," *San Francisco Chronicle Sunday Magazine,* October 22, 1967, 37.

8. Richard A. Reuss, "Woody Guthrie and His Folk Tradition," *The Journal of American Folklore,* vol. 83, no. 329, July–Sept. 1970, 296.

9. Richard A. Reuss, comp., *Woody Guthrie: Bibliography* (New York: The Guthrie Children's Trust Fund, 1968), i, iii.

10. John Greenway, "Woodrow Wilson Guthrie (1912–1967)," *The Journal of American Folklore,* vol. 81, no. 319, Jan.-Mar. 1968, 63–64.

11. Alan Lomax, Woody Guthrie, Pete Seeger, *Hard Hitting Songs for Hard-Hit People* (New York: Oak Publications, 1967), 12.

12. Herbert Russcol, "I gave my love a cherry, tell it like it is, baby!," *High Fidelity,* vol. 18, December 1968, 55, 58.

13. "Notes," *Broadside,* #89, February-March 1968.

14. Robert Shelton, "Tribute to the Life and Legend of Woody Guthrie," *New York Times,* Janu-

ary 22, 1968, 31; Woody Guthrie, "Dear Mrs. Roosevelt," Harold Leventhal and Marjorie Guthrie, *The Woody Guthrie Songbook* (New York: Grosset & Dunlap, 1976), 71.

15. Ellen Willis, "A Tribute to Woody Guthrie," *Cheetah,* March 1968, 19; Clive Davis, *Clive: Inside the Record Business* (New York: Ballantine, 1976), 68–69.

16. Eli Jaffe, "Woody Guthrie/A Remembrance," *Broadside,* #89, February-Mach 1968.

17. Robert Hilburn, "Tribute to Woody Guthrie," *Los Angeles Times,* September 14, 1970, E1.

18. Millard Lampell, "Hard Travelin'," *A Tribute To Woody Guthrie* (New York: Woody Guthrie Publications, 1972), 2–3.

19. "Tribute," *New Yorker,* January 29, 1972, 31.

20. http://www.countryjoe.com/guthrie.htm (2011)

21. Ellen Willis, "Newport: You Can't Go Down Home Again," *New Yorker,* August 17, 1968, 90.

22. Nat Hentoff, "Woody Guthrie Still Prowls Our Memories," *New York Times,* April 16, 1972, D28.

23. Jean Heller, "Woody Guthrie Wins Hearts Of Hundreds," *Freelance-Star* (Fredericksburg, Virginia), April 25, 1966, 2; Henrietta Yurchenco assisted by Marjorie Guthrie, *A Mighty Hard Road: The Woody Guthrie Story* (New York: McGraw-Hill Book Co., 1970), 12–13.

24. Woody Guthrie, *Woody Sez* (New York: Grosset & Dunlap, 1975), vii, ix–x.

25. Harold Leventhal and Marjorie Guthrie, eds., *The Woody Guthrie Songbook* (New York: Grosset & Dunlap, 1976), 14, 26

26. Woody Guthrie, *Seeds Of Man: An Experiment Lived and Dreamed* (New York: E. P. Dutton & Co., 1976), 7.

27. Marsha Meyer, "Woody Guthrie: The Legend Lives," *Wax Paper,* vol. 1, no. 2, December 28, 1976, 26–27.

28. Moses Asch, liner notes, *Struggle,* Folkways Records FA 2485, 1976.

29. Federick Turner, "'Just What In the Hell Has Gone Wrong Here Anyhow?' Woody Guthrie And the American Dream," *American Heritage Magazine,* vol. 28, issue 6, October 1977, http://www.americanheritage.com.

30. Joe Klein, *Woody Guthrie: A Life* (New York: Alfred A. Knopf, 1980), xvi.

31. Joe Klein, "Woody's Children," *Esquire,* vol. 94, no. 4, October 1980, 76.

32. Murray Kempton, "The Curse of the Guthries," *The New York Review of Books,* February 19, 1981, 8, 10, 11.

33. Jon Pareles, "Woody Guthrie: Hard Travelin'," *New York Times,* March 7, 1984.

34. Dave Marsh, "Introduction," Dave Marsh and Harold Leventhal, eds., *Pastures Of Plenty: A Self-Portrait, Woody Guthrie* (New York: HarperCollins Publishers, 1990), xviii–xix, xxii.

35. Ralph Rinzler, Foreword," Will Schmid, *A Tribute to Woody Guthrie & Leadbelly: Teacher's Guide* (Reston, VA: Music Educators National Conference, 1991), 4.

36. Michael Gallucci, "Guthrie Honored at Hall of Fame Ceremony," *Goldmine,* December 6, 1996.

37. Springsteen quoted in Frank E. Pointer, "Woody Guthrie; aka 'The guy who wrote "This Land Is Your Land,"'" John Partington, ed., *The Life, Music and Thought of Woody Guthrie: A Critical Appraisal* (Reading: Ashgate Publishing Ltd., 2011), 123.

38. Robert Santell, "Preface," Robert Santelli and Emily Davidson, eds., *Hard Travelin': The Life and Legacy of Woody Guthrie* (Hanover: Wesleyan University Press, 1999), xi.

39. Dave Marsh, "Deportees: Woody Guthrie's Unfinished Business," Santelli and Davidson, eds., *Hard Travelin,* 173, 177–178.

40. Steve Earle, "Christmas In Washington," *El Corazón,* Warner Bros., B000002NIC, 1997.

41. Peter Applebome, "New Glimpses of Woody Guthrie's Imagination," *New York Times,* April 27, 1998.

42. Applebome, "New Glimpses of Woody Guthrie's Imagination," *New York Times,* April 27, 1998.

43. Billy Bragg, liner notes, Billy Bragg & Wilco, *Mermaid Avenue,* Elektra, 62204-2, 1998; Applebome, "New Glimpses of Woody Guthrie's Imagination."

44. Robert Christgau, "Pop/Jazz; What if Woody Guthrie Had Led a Rock Band?," *New York Times,* June 28, 1998; Nick Krewen, "The Other Side of a Folk Legend," *Toronto Star,* July 27, 1998.

45. Billy Bragg, liner notes, Billy Bragg & Wilco, *Mermaid Avenue Vol. II,* Elektra, 62522-2, 2000.

46. Jon Pareles, "Music Review; Funny, Woody, You Don't Look Klezmer," *New York Times,* December 23, 2003.

47. Vivien Goldman, liner notes, The Klezmatics, *Wonder Wheel: Lyrics By Woody Guthrie,* Jewish Music Group, JMG 18033-2, 2006.

48. Moses Asch, "The Ballad of Chanuka," *Sing Out!,* vol. 17, no. 6, December/January 1967/68, 12.

49. Nora Guthrie, "His Pure Love of People," Program, *Nashville Sings Woody at the Ryman,* 2003.

50. Geoffrey Himes, "This land is country," *No Depression,* March–April 1998, 92.

51. Steven Brower & Nora Guthrie, *Woody Guthrie: Art Works* (New York: Rizzoli, 9.

52. Nora Guthrie, liner notes, 9, Woody Guthrie, *My Dusty Road,* Rounder Records 2009.

53. Jay Lustig, "Fanfare for an uncommon man," (Newark) *Sunday Star-Ledger,* November 16, 2003.

54. Geoffrey Himes, "Dead 40 Years, Woody Guthrie Stays Busy," *New York Times,* September 2, 2007.

55. David King Dunaway and Molly Beer, *Singing Out: An Oral History of America's Folk Music Revivals* (New York: Oxford University Press, 2010), 187–188.

56. Richard Carlin, *Worlds of Sound: The Story of Smithsonian Folkways* (New York: Smithsonian Books/Collins, 2008), 44–45.

57. Joan Anderman, "Unearthed in a Brooklyn basement, a trove of Woody Guthrie recordings will see the light in a new four-CD collection—and he's never sounded better," *Boston Globe,* August 2, 2009.

58. Dorian Lynskey, *33 Revolutions Per MInute: A History of Protest Songs, From Billie Holiday to Green Day* (New York: Ecco, 2011), 15.

59. Pete Seeger, *The Incomplete Folksinger,* ed. Jo Metcalf Schwartz (New York: Simon and Schuster, 1972), 58, 60.

BIBLIOGRAPHY

A Tribute to Woody Guthrie. New York: Woody Guthrie Publications, 1972.

Bray, Thelma. *Reflections: The Life and Times of Woody Guthrie*. Pampa: Thelma Bray, 2002.

Brower, Steven and Nora Guthrie. *Woody Guthrie: Art Works*. New York: Rizzoli, 2005.

Carlin, Richard. *Worlds of Sound: The Story of Smithsonian Folkways*. New York: Smithsonian Books/Collins, 2008.

Cohen, Ronald D., ed., *Alan Lomax, Assistant in Charge: The Library of Congress Letters 1935–1945*. Jackson: University Press of Mississippi, 2011.

Cohen, Ronald D. *Rainbow Quest: The Folk Music Revival and American Society, 1940–1970*. Amherst: University of Massachusetts Press, 2002.

Cray, Ed. *Ramblin' Man: The Life and Times of Woody Guthrie*. New York: W. W. Norton & Co., 2004.

Cunningham, Agnes "Sis" and Gordon Friesen. *Red Dust and Broadsides: A Joint Autobiography*. Amherst: University of Massachusetts Press, 1999.

Denning, Michael. *The Cultural Front: The Laboring of American Culture in the Twentieth Century*. New York: Verso, 1996.

Every 100 Years Songbook. New York: TRO-The Richmond Organization, 2011.

Goggans Jan. *California on the Breadlines: Dorothea Lange, Paul Taylor, and the Making of a New Deal Narrative*. Berkeley: University of California Press, 2010.

Golio, Gary and Marc Burkhardt. *When Bob Met Woody: The Story of the Young Bob Dylan*. New York: Little, Brown and Company, 2011.

Greenway, John, *American Folk Songs of Protest*. Philadelphia: University of Pennsylvania Press, 1953.

Guthrie, Mary Jo and Guy Logsdon. *Woody's Road: Woody Guthrie's Letters Home, Drawings, Photos, and Other Unburied Treasures*. Boulder, CO: Paradigm Publishers, 2012.

Guthrie, Nora and The Woody Guthrie Archives. *My Name Is New York: Ramblin' Around Woody Guthrie's New York Town: A Walking Guide*. New York: PowerHouse Books, 2012.

Guthrie, Woody. *Seeds Of Man: An Experiment Lived and Dreamed*. New York: E. P. Dutton & Co., 1976.

Guthrie, Woody. *Woody Sez*. New York: Grosset & Dunlap, 1975.

Guthrie, Woody. *Born To Win*. Ed. Robert Shelton. New York: Collier Books, 1967.

Guthrie, Woody. *Bound For Glory*. New York: E. P. Dutton & Co., 1943.

Guthrie, Woody with Marjorie Mazia Guthrie. *Woody's 20 Grow Big Songs*. New York: HarperCollins, 1992.

Hawes, Bess Lomax. *Sing It Pretty: A Memoir*. Urbana: University of Illinois Press, 2008.

Jackson, Mark Allan. *Prophet Singer: The Voice and Vision of Woody Guthrie*. Jackson: University Press of Mississippi, 2007.

Klein, Joe. *Woody Guthrie: A Life*. New York: Alfred A. Knopf, 1980.

Kaufman, Will. *Woody Guthrie, American Radical*. Urbana: University of Illinois Press, 2011.

La Chapelle, Peter. *Proud To Be An Okie: Cultural Politics, Country Music, and Migration To Southern California*. Berkeley: University of California Press, 2007.

Leventhal, Harold and Marjorie Guthrie, eds. *The Woody Guthrie Songbook*. New York: Grosset & Dunlap, 1976.

Longhi, Jim. *Woody, Cisco, & Me: Seamen Three in the Merchant Marine*. Urbana: University of Illinois Press, 1997.

Marsh, Dave and Harold Leventhal, eds. *Pastures of Plenty: A Self-Portrait, Woody Guthrie*. New York: HarperCollins, 1990.

Partington, John S., ed. *The LIfe, Music and Thought of Woody Guthrie: A Critical Appraisal*. Farnham, England: Ashgate, 2011.

Partridge, Elizabeth. *This Land Was Made for You and Me: The Life & Songs of Woody Guthrie*. New York: Viking, 2002.

Place, Jeff and Robert Santelli. *Woody At 100*. 4 cds plus a large book. Washington, D.C.: Smithsonian Folkways 40200, 2012.

Reineke, Hank. *Ramblin' Jack Elliott: The Never-Ending Highway*. Lanham, MD: The Scarecrow Press, 2010.

Reuss, Richard A. with JoAnne C. Reuss. *American Folk Music and Left-Wing Politics, 1927–1957*. Lanham, MD: The Scarecrow Press, 2000.

Robbin, Ed. *Woody Guthrie and Me*. Berkeley; Lancaster-Miller Publishers, 1979.

Santelli, Robert. *This Land Is Your Land: Woody Guthrie and the Journey of the American Folk Song*. New York: Running Press, 2012.

Santelli, Robert and Emily Davidson, eds. *Hard Travelin': The LIfe and Legacy of Woody Guthrie*. Hanover: Wesleyan University Press, 1999.

Shelton, Robert. *No Direction Home: The Life and Music of Bob Dylan*. New York: William Morrow, 1986.

Szwed, John. *Alan Lomax: The Man Who Recorded the World*. New York: Viking, 2010.

Yurchenco, Henrietta assisted by Marjorie Guthrie. *A Mighty Hard Road: The Woody Guthrie Story*. New York: McGraw-Hill, 1970.

INDEX